YSL.COM

THE
PITCHFORK
REVIEW

We've got issues.

CONTRIBUTORS

Charles Aaron
Demi Adejuyigbe
Molly Beauchemin
Alexis Beauclair
Janette Beckman
Joseph Bien-Kahn
Sara Bivigou
Ryan Dombal
Sara Drake
Meaghan Garvey
Lea Heinrich
Beth Hoeckel
Jeff Johnson
Tim Kinsella
Hannah K. Lee
Zoë Leverant
Peter Margasak
Anders Nilsen

J.R. Nelson
Louise Pomeroy
T. Cole Rachel
Ron Regé Jr.
Marianna Ritchey
John Roberts
David Roth
Scott Seward
David C. Sampson
Johnny Sampson
Eric Shorey
Jes Skolnik
Laura Snapes
Hattie Stewart
Eric Torres
Dan Trombly
Elijah Wald
Barry Walters

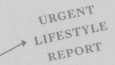
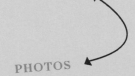

ISSUE No.

The Pitchfork Review No. 7, Summer 2015. Published
four times a year by Pitchfork Media Inc., 3317 W.
Fullerton Ave., Chicago, IL 60647. All material ©
2015. All rights reserved. Subscription rate in the
US for 4 issues is $49.99. The Pitchfork Review is
distributed by Publishers Group West. All advertising
inquiries should be directed to Matthew Frampton
at mattf@pitchfork.com. The Pitchfork Review does
not read or accept unsolicited submissions, nor does
it assume responsibility for the views expressed by its
contributors. Contact info@thepitchforkreview.com
for general information and reprints. Reproduction
in whole or in part without permission is prohibited.
The Pitchfork Review is a registered trademark of
Pitchfork Media Inc.

Printed by Palmer Printing Inc. 739 S. Clark St.,
Chicago, IL 60605. Set in typefaces from Klim Type
Foundry (klim.co.nz), Lineto (lineto.com), Colophon
Foundry (colophon-foundry.org), Grilli Type (grillitype.
com), and Mergenthaler. Printed on Mohawk Via and
porcelainECO from Veritev.

ISBN 978-0-9913992-6-0

ABOUT THE COVER
Photo: Grace Jones for *A View to a Kill*, by John Glen
Art by Hattie Stewart

Ryan Schreiber
Founder & CEO

Chris Kaskie
President

Michael Renaud
Vice President

Ryan Kennedy
Publisher

Jessica Hopper
Editor in Chief

Michael Catano
Deputy Editor

Naomi Huffman
Oriana Leckert
Proofreaders

Ameila Dobmeyer
Operations

Molly Raskin
General Manager

Danielle Pierre
Support

Molly Butterfoss
Art Director

Joy Burke
Jessica Viscius
Graphic Design

Erik Sanchez
*Photo Editor
(Contributing)*

Christian Storm
*Photo Editor
(Contributing)*

Matthew Frampton
VP, Business

Megan Davey
VP, Finance

Charlotte Zoller
Social Media

RJ Bentler
*VP, Video
Programming*

Ash Slater
Events & Support

Matthew Dennewitz
VP, Product

Mark Beasley
Andrew Gaerig
Neil Wargo
Developers

Ryan Dombal
Mark Richardson
Brandon Stosuy
Editorial

Putting musicians on the cover of *The Pitchfork Review* wasn't really something we ever intended to do.

But Grace Jones is special. Part of what has made her an icon for so many is her ability to reflect back, amplify, and validate the needs of her listeners and admirers. The nature of her power, her transgression, and perhaps even her womanhood depends entirely on who is beholding her—who is shouting "Pull up to my bumper, baby!" in the middle of a crowded dance floor. In Barry Walters' cover story for this issue, Jones is the diva singing queer truths that cannot be spoken aloud. She's the Queen of the Freaks, but we also see her as a driven artist who spends $385,000 perfecting "Slave to the Rhythm."

As enrapturing as she and her albums are, discussions of Grace Jones let us to talk about so much else, race, gender, disco, about who we are, what music allows that culture does not, and most importantly of all about who we become in the light of another's song.

—*Jessica Hopper, Editor in Chief*

flipbait

Flipbait is the section of the Review where your favorite team makes the winning catch!

ALL ILLUSTRATIONS BY *RON REGÉ, JR*

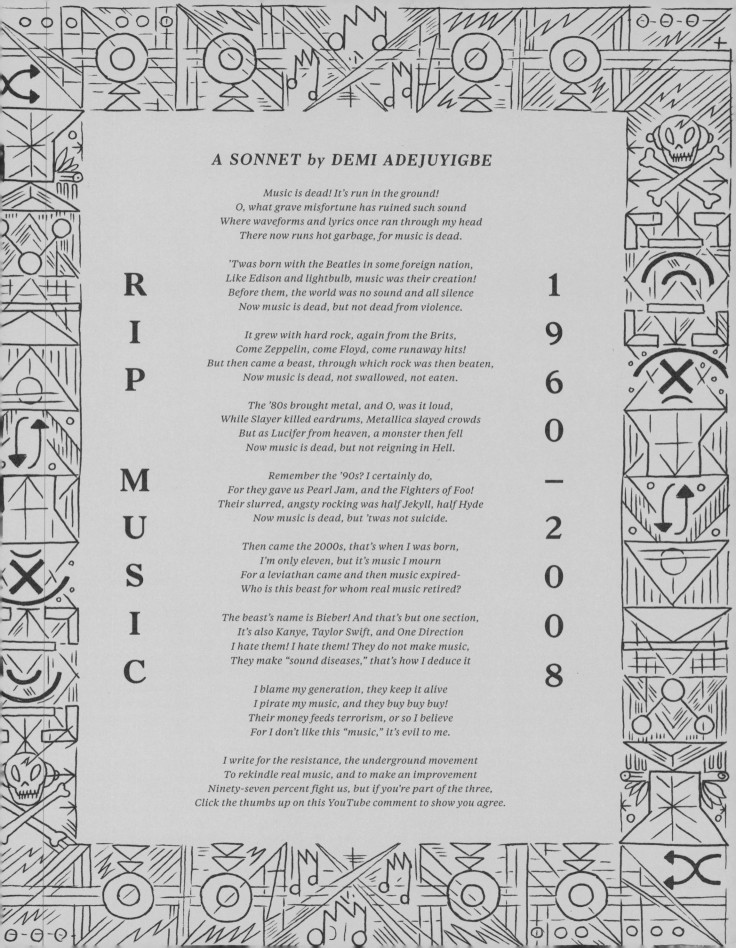

A SONNET by DEMI ADEJUYIGBE

Music is dead! It's run in the ground!
O, what grave misfortune has ruined such sound
Where waveforms and lyrics once ran through my head
There now runs hot garbage, for music is dead.

'Twas born with the Beatles in some foreign nation,
Like Edison and lightbulb, music was their creation!
Before them, the world was no sound and all silence
Now music is dead, but not dead from violence.

It grew with hard rock, again from the Brits,
Come Zeppelin, come Floyd, come runaway hits!
But then came a beast, through which rock was then beaten,
Now music is dead, not swallowed, not eaten.

The '80s brought metal, and O, was it loud,
While Slayer killed eardrums, Metallica slayed crowds
But as Lucifer from heaven, a monster then fell
Now music is dead, but not reigning in Hell.

Remember the '90s? I certainly do,
For they gave us Pearl Jam, and the Fighters of Foo!
Their slurred, angsty rocking was half Jekyll, half Hyde
Now music is dead, but 'twas not suicide.

Then came the 2000s, that's when I was born,
I'm only eleven, but it's music I mourn
For a leviathan came and then music expired-
Who is this beast for whom real music retired?

The beast's name is Bieber! And that's but one section,
It's also Kanye, Taylor Swift, and One Direction
I hate them! I hate them! They do not make music,
They make "sound diseases," that's how I deduce it

I blame my generation, they keep it alive
I pirate my music, and they buy buy buy!
Their money feeds terrorism, or so I believe
For I don't like this "music," it's evil to me.

I write for the resistance, the underground movement
To rekindle real music, and to make an improvement
Ninety-seven percent fight us, but if you're part of the three,
Click the thumbs up on this YouTube comment to show you agree.

R
I
P

M
U
S
I
C

1
9
6
0
–
2
0
0
8

Great Hunks of Music History: Franz Liszt

The original rock star or glove-peeling cad?

The term "Romanticism" conjures up a rich welter of adjectives and images in anyone who has studied the history of art, music, and/or poetry. We picture Caspar David Friedrich's *Wanderer Above the Sea of Fog*, which depicts a lone gentleman gazing out over the inconceivable vastness of God's creation, emotionally stirred but—thanks to his finely honed intellectual sensitivity and strong sense of self—uncowed, and even empowered, by the sublime encounter. We think of Byron, extolling the virtues of the outsider, the solitary artist-hero too brilliant, too sensitive to engage in the mundane activities of bourgeois society. Europeans' belief in individual rights—which had been percolating since the Renaissance—coalesced in the explosion of Democratic ideals that undergirded the French Revolution. That the pure humanistic goals of the Enlightenment turned so quickly into totalitarian violence (there were only three years between the fall of the Bastille and the beginning of the Reign of Terror, in which the gutters of Paris and Lyons were clogged with the bloody runoff from the guillotine) led to a sort of world-weary cynicism in the next generation, who tended to be suspicious of governments and of mass culture, obsessed with severed heads and other macabre images, and who increasingly turned inward in the search for truth and coherence. Hence

Friedrich's *Wanderer*, proudly isolated and self-contained atop his craggy peak.

The fetish for individualism that characterizes Romantic art can be seen in a number of themes that appear again and again in the era. There are the obvious tropes of lone men standing on mountaintops or brooding gloomily on cliff edges, but there is also the rise of the bildungsroman, which privileges individual experience and struggle in the creation of a fully actualized human subject. There's Beethoven's symphonic transformation of the musical structure of "sonata form" to mirror that struggle-to-triumph narrative, and, more to our present purposes, there's the enormous emphasis in nineteenth century music on a new kind of virtuosity, one founded less on the desire to delight and please—as in the sparkling and witty *stile brillante* deployed by previous prodigies like Mozart—than on the imperative to shock and even horrify the massed audience swooning at the virtuoso's feet.

In the Romantic Era, the preferred manner of demonstrating the technical dexterity that was considered the hallmark of virtuosity involved not only extended techniques and avant-garde dissonances but also a sort of grotesque intensity described by some observers as "demonic." The great violinist Paganini, for example, intentionally left his dentures out whenever he performed, so that his already cadaverous face (he was made hideous by disease early in life) would appear even more sunken and appalling, and he grew his hair out long, so that he could fling it wildly around onstage. Paganini is depicted in contemporary illustrations as cartoonishly gaunt and haggard, with flames and smoke spouting from the instrument tucked underneath his pockmarked chin. In the nineteenth century vogue for demonic, otherworldly virtuoso performers, we can see the individualism fetish writ large, literally plastered all over town in concert advertisements: *Come see the man who has done nothing for his entire life but practice his scales! Verily, he cares nothing for fashion or appearance, commerce or education, the society of his fellows, the wool trade, or whatever vapid Donizetti monstrosity they're putting on at the Opéra! He cares only for the Great Art that lives in his soul alone!* The audiences that flocked to see Paganini shred onstage were really paying for the privilege of witnessing a True Individual at work, as though the concert hall had become some sort of World's Fair exhibit in reverse, with the "savages" gawking at an "advanced" culture, instead of the other way around.

A twenty-one-year-old Franz Liszt saw Paganini perform in 1832 and experienced an epiphany that was to have major ramifications on the history of Western art music. Liszt, up to that point, had been a piano virtuoso in the old school style, playing clever, glistening cascades of notes and twinkling trills for audiences who rewarded him with genteel applause. But after being exposed to Paganini's gnomic capering, and the sublime awe and terror that his strange mixture of ugliness and genius inspired, Liszt decided to change his entire life and become a precursor to the modern rock star. He canceled all his performance dates and went into seclusion. He tore his own painstakingly acquired technique down to nothing and rebuilt it from scratch, seeking to emulate and explore Paganini's violin techniques on the piano. Through this painful, bildungsroman-esque personal journey, Liszt ultimately became the most celebrated pianist of his—or really any—era.

A huge part of Liszt's fame, though, had to do with his public image. This is why I declare him—and not Paganini—to be the first true rock star, because, while Liszt modeled his playing after Paganini, his public image was of his own design. Paganini's appearance and stage presence was just a bit too weird, too ugly, for him to ever completely transcend the whiff of the freak-show that always hung around him. Leigh Hunt famously went to great lengths to dehumanize Paganini in his glowing review, noting that his face is "like a mask" and saying several times that he only appears to be truly alive when he is playing the violin. He compares Paganini to not one but *three* different non-human beasts—"he bows like a camel, and grins like a goblin or a mountain-goat."

None of this could quite be said of Liszt, because no amount of onstage shenanigans could obscure his extreme hunkiness. When you look at drawings and photographs of the great composers, there really are very few obvious babes. Beethoven, with his constant glower and his earthy humanity, is more sensual than sexy—one imagines him reeking of beer and sausages and falling asleep on top of oneself mid-coitus. Mozart looks like a small child no matter what age he is. There's a cute sweetness in Schubert's bespectacled face and close-cropped curly hair, but then again, he would have been covered with syphilis sores and mercury burns for most of his adult life, and he was a shy performer to boot. Chopin was gaunt, pale, and constantly on his deathbed. Clara Schumann had huge stage presence and was a serious babe, but her vibe was pretty goth. And don't even get me started on the postwar modernists. With their enormous haunted eyes and brutal frowns, they all look like Munch's "The Scream," although of course you can't blame them. So when it comes to the kind of gleaming, bare-chested, transcendently joyous, narcissistically macho sex appeal we associate with the true rock stars of the '60s and '70s—your Daltreys, your Plants—the only real precursor is Liszt.

He used his good looks to his advantage, but more importantly, he combined them with the type of stage presence and public image that was conducive to worship, at a time of heroic individuality. He played to his audiences, giving them what they wanted to see: a guy blisteringly shredding on the piano, making it seem like the notes were spontaneously pouring from him (rather than the truth, which was that he had to practice almost constantly to attain his level of technical skill), his eyes closed, his thoughts directed inward, his superior sensitivity finding its authentic expression only within his own being, etc.—But then he'd do stuff like erotically peel off a glove and hurl it into the audience while women shrieked and tore at their bosoms. There are countless contemporary drawings of Liszt concerts that look like depictions of riots: people screaming, men catching innumerable swooning women in their arms and racing from the room like firefighters from a conflagration. In short, it was Beatlemania with lower hemlines and, actually, even longer hair.

I've been learning about Liszt for what feels like my whole life. He's the "Good Vibrations" of classical music history—a touchstone that feels like it perfectly manifests all the interests and issues of its time, a watershed moment after which nothing will ever be the same, blah blah blah—which I tend to take with a grain of salt, as of course these things often loom larger in hindsight than they did at their own time. So you can imagine my delight at reading Robert and Clara Schumann's marriage diaries and finding that they describe Liszt as I always pictured him. Here is Clara:

After the concert we had dinner together in the evening at Heinrich Brockhaus's—there wasn't much to be done with Liszt, since 2 ladies had taken possession of him. I'm convinced that women generally are at fault when Liszt sometimes shows himself to be very arrogant, since they pay court to him everywhere in ways that I detest, which I also find highly indecent. I worship him too, but even veneration must have a limit. I'm gossiping, isn't that true dear Robert, pardon! Give me a slap—!

The differences between them are striking. The Schumanns are always tired; they've got a million babies and they enjoy their domestic life, and too much noise is hard on Robert's nerves. They're both always having to spend the day lying down in a dark room because they're too depressed or feverish. Liszt, on the other hand, is always out all night, showing up with babes he brought from another party, drinking all the champagne in the house, just kind of being his own dude, marching very much to the beat of his own drum (individualism!). Here's Clara again:

On Thursday the 16th Liszt played for the last time... He seemed tired out, which with his life-style is not

surprising—he didn't arrive from Halle, where he had caroused all night, until early in the morning, and still held 3 rehearsals before noon.

In the marriage diaries, both Robert and Clara express a sort of exasperated veneration of Liszt that is interesting when one thinks of how history has placed them at such odds. The Schumanns were very conservative; they wanted to keep writing Beethovenian symphonies, basically, while weirdos like Wagner and Liszt thought that Beethoven himself had exhausted the genre of instrumental music, and that the only way forward was to return to texts and programs. Clara herself, of course, was a great and internationally beloved virtuoso, but her conservative attitude probably prevented her from capitalizing so explosively on sex appeal. Perhaps her gender also prevented this, although it's worth remembering that women opera singers at the time were 100 percent able to express a similar kind of self-centered, loud sexiness as Liszt. Anyway, history puts Liszt and the Schumanns on opposite sides of a rancorous battle for the future of music, but in the diaries, they're clearly all pals, or at least they were in the 1850s. It's clear, in fact, that for the Schumanns there were two different Liszts. Liszt the player was very different from Liszt the composer, who drove them crazy. Here is Clara, yet again:

≡✳

When you look at drawings and photographs
of the great composers, there really are very few
obvious babes. Beethoven, with his constant glower
and his earthy humanity, is more sensual than sexy—
one imagines him reeking of beer and sausages and
falling asleep on top of oneself mid-coitus.

Liszt may play as he wants, it is always spirited, even if tasteless at times, of which one can accuse his compositions especially; I can't call them anything but abominable—a chaos of dissonances, the shrillest, a ceaseless murmuring in the deepest bass combined with the highest treble, boring introductions, etc. As a composer I could almost hate him.

Boring introductions! It's interesting because we forget that Liszt was a famous performer for quite some time before he started doing the kind of innovative composition that got him booed at Leipzig. He didn't really start shaking up the compositional world until he quit performing altogether when he was thirty-five and moved to Weimar, which shocked everyone because Weimar was kind of a burg, not at all the artistic party capital (Paris) you'd have expected Liszt to settle down in. It was a little bit like if, in 1988, Eddie Van Halen had quit playing in a band, moved to Colorado Springs, and suddenly started putting out Björk albums.

It's fascinating to read Clara's thoughts on Liszt, as they were more or less professional equals (Clara's characteristic self-deprecation notwithstanding) and no doubt had a mutual understanding of the difficulties, the anguish, of being famous touring pianists, which few others at the time could share. When some random journalist describes Liszt's playing as "sublime," it could mean anything—it could mean that he played really well, or it could just mean that it was fashionable to declare such a thing. When Clara describes Liszt's playing, though, we are getting more of an honest portrait:

> But as a player in his concert...he astonished me extremely and especially in the Don Juan Fantasy, which he played rapturously—his performance of the champagne aria will remain unforgettable for me, this wantonness, the joy with which he played, it was unique!

In the nineteenth century, age thirty five was fully middle-aged, so I imagine that once he was at Weimar, Liszt's flamboyant performance energy was channelled into the more cerebral pursuits of composing and rigorously training his in-house orchestra in the kinds of extended techniques required to play the newest, hippest music. His handsome youth slowly transformed into a an elegant, streamlined old age. His daughter married Wagner. He fell down a flight of stairs. At last, in 1886, at the cusp of a new century, he died a wild-haired old man of seventy-five. And so concludes the tale of one of history's great hunks. ✎

Excerpts from: *The Marriage Diaries of Robert and Clara Schumann: From Their Wedding Day to the Russia Trip.* By: Gerd Nauhaus & Peter F. Ostwald (translator)

WHO WORE IT BETTER
(On the Album Cover)?

by Zoë Leverant

Forget *Us Weekly*; the hottest style standoffs are in the record bins. Whether ripoffs or coincidences, these pairs are going toe-to-toe for the title of best-similarly-dressed.

FUTURE ISLANDS
Singles

NEUTRAL MILK HOTEL
In the Aeroplane Over the Sea

THE VERDICT

Headless Dress On Seaside is a classic choice, and while *Aeroplane* Lady may have looked groundbreaking in 1998, her heavy antique frock comes off as dated and tone-deaf for today's budget-minded cover models living in climate change heat. *Singles* Lady's more lightweight and understated take is the perfect update, and she looks stunning in those bold stripes.

ST. VINCENT
St. Vincent

THEESATISFACTION
EarthEE

THE VERDICT

The imperial space age future trend is so yesterday, but that didn't keep both St. Vincent and THEESatisfaction from trying it on. Sadly Annie just doesn't go far enough, and she winds up looking more 1970s than 2070s. Stas and Cat get it totally right with their stylishly risqué translucent royal uniforms, which manage to be both retro and fashion-forward.

HUNX & HIS PUNX
Gay Singles

PEACHES
The Teaches of Peaches

THE VERDICT

They're here, they're queer, get used to their album covers: Hunx and Peaches rock outfits as confrontational as their music. While Hunx's prolific leg hair gets kudos, he's too over-the-top to come out on top. Peaches' subtly jarring undies—are they see-through or not?—are seductive and weird in all the right ways. Deliberately unpretty in pink is the way to go.

SUFJAN STEVENS
The Avalanche

RAGE AGAINST THE MACHINE *Evil Empire*

THE VERDICT

These two hardly run in the same circles, but they stepped out in such similar ensembles they've become fashion frenemies. Captain Evil's statement red easily makes his look the better one, living up to his heroic aims. Doctor Avalanche, on the other hand, belongs with the outtakes he's repping. Sorry, Sufjan. Leave the capes to the experts.

BELLE & SEBASTIAN
Tigermilk

CAMERA OBSCURA
Underachievers Please Try Harder

THE VERDICT

Meet the hottest accessory in the twee-verse: soft stuffed animals. The Obscura girls keep it cute and pulled together, perfectly matching beret colors to their adorable furry friend. Coordinated as they might be, though, Miss Belle's sweet but sexy style steals the show in the end. She and her bosom buddy make quite the stylish pair. Sometimes, the original can't be beat.

SPRING EDITION
BY J.R. NELSON

READING LIST

*Country Soul: Making Music and Race
in the American South*
by Charles L. Hughes
(2015, University of North Carolina Press)

Circulation Desk

The racial dynamics of where Country and Soul met

You might have seen the advertisement during the time out commercial break on a football Sunday (like I did), or maybe after an episode of *Grey's Anatomy*, and still remembered it years later. Five middle-aged black women are on stage in a darkened, teeming nightclub, performing the instantly-identifiable opening chords of the Staple Singers' "I'll Take You There;" an almost note-perfect cover, so very near to the song's vision of sweetest eternity and racial transcendence in heaven (if not quite here on earth) as to be almost identical. The fabled Chicago family's funky gospel soul smash charged to No. 1 in 1972 for Memphis soul label Stax, and soon topped literally every record chart known to mankind, arguably becoming the Staples' and Stax's biggest hit. But there is an irony: the backing musicians are almost all white; although Mavis Staples implores each of the family's members to solo, including Roebuck "Pops" Staples on guitar, white members of the Muscle Shoals Rhythm Section respond. As pure musical symbolism, the glowing gospel strains and powerful rolling groove of "I'll Take You There"—recorded in the cradle of the American south in Memphis, Tennessee—has, to many Americans, come to represent the unstoppable force of racial conciliation and national redemption, much like the rare interracial milieu from which it stemmed, where musicians steeped in rhythm and blues and gospel and country came together to craft a new language of song. Mavis Staples performed "I'll Take You There" at the White House in 2013 as part of a Memphis Soul celebration broadcast on PBS, and you could hardly miss the First Family dancing in their seats and eagerly singing along to each other in the front row, or the white and black musicians seamlessly playing together on stage.

Stated plainly, the classic southern soul era—which spans much of the '60s and early '70s—provides a litany of musical talent and a culture-enriching wealth of dizzying listening pleasure. It was birthed from a time of incredible bravery, pain, and chaos, sewn by a cast of hundreds who often couldn't eat together or stay at the same hotels: backing bands like the integrated Booker T and the M.G.'s, the all-white "Swampers" of the Muscle Shoals Rhythm Section, and the Bar-Kays. The dynamic, blazing voices of the great black singers: Otis Redding, Joe Tex, Wilson Pickett, Sam and Dave, Percy Sledge, Carla Thomas, and Candi Staton. The genius songwriters, black and white: David Porter and Issac Hayes, Spooner Oldham and Dan Penn. The white studio founders and record executives: Rick Hall at FAME in Muscle Shoals and Estelle Axton and Jim Stewart at Stax in Memphis. With society outside the walls of the recording studio rocked by white intransigence as blacks searched for the barest modicum of racial and economic justice, it's incredible that inside the studio, blacks and whites worked alongside one another as equals, providing a musical backdrop for the landmark victories of the Civil Rights era.

This narrative was established through record label, recording studio, and even civic promotional campaigns of the era, and has been cemented in books like Peter Guralnick's *Sweet Soul Music: Rhythm and Blues and the Southern Dream of Freedom*, as well as documentary films like *Respect Yourself:*

The Stax Records Story and Muscle Shoals. And it only seem to increase in allure and cultural selling power as the era fades into the distance.

However, in his exceptional new book Country Soul: Making Music and Making Race In The American South, Oklahoma State University history professor Charles L. Hughes digs deep into the racial and labor politics of the time—a recording studio job is still a job, after all—and reveals that despite decades of scholarship on this golden narrative of easy musical togetherness, a frustratingly persistent and predictable inequality along racial lines remains largely unexamined. As Hughes argues, "African American musicians consistently objected to mistreatment from whites and worked to equalize the racial dynamics of southern studios from the very beginning."

As its title suggests, Country Soul broadens the typical geographic binary of black-identified soul sounds to include Nashville. There, white musicians could augment their income and seek opportunities for musical collaboration with far more ease than their black associates, even as their cross-pollination of soul and country began to flower. In this respect, the book is vastly illuminating. Hughes offers a litany of evidence that "country and soul records were made by the same people, recorded in the same places, and released by the same record companies. Indeed, even as the genres became opposites in the national consciousness, they were inextricably linked on the production level [...] the relationship between country and soul was the South—and the United States—in microcosm." Indeed, Hughes carries this thread even further,

examining the "New Right" conservative backlash inherent in country music that emerged even before the Civil Rights era had come close to finishing. Reactionary hits like Terry Nelson's "The Battle Hymn of Lt. Calley" (an eerily-impassioned and deeply ignorant defense of William Calley, the Vietnam veteran who instigated the My Lai massacre, where several hundred unarmed Vietnamese civilians were executed by trigger happy soldiers) were backed by musical talent on loan from Muscle Shoals.

Hughes' book illuminates several disparate characters whose careers were buffeted by these economic and racial forces. Charley Pride, the first and still one of the few true black country superstars, was hidden in plain sight as his career began, and spent the rest of it attesting to color blindness as he crafted

a brilliant singing career. Producer Chet Atkins originally kept Pride's picture from record sleeves and promotional materials before "securing radio play and record sales." Only then did "Atkins and Pride reveal that the young star was African American." According to Hughes, "Pride's success and devotion to the rhetoric of color blindness offered a microcosm of both the possibilities and limits of country's gestures toward racial progressivism [...] the only African American who achieved major country stardom in this period was someone who explicitly and implicitly distanced himself from racial confrontation and whose racially motivated criticisms were almost always directed toward other blacks."

Producer, singer, songwriter, and provocateur Jerry "Swamp Dogg" Williams straddled the whole of the country/soul paradigm like few others. In Hughes' telling, "early exposure gave Williams a love for country that predated his appreciation for music more habitually identified with African Americans." Although Williams had R&B hits such as "Little Jerry Williams" in the mid-'60s and even became the first black staff producer at Atlantic Records (by his own account he felt like a token hire and never truly found his place at the label), he's always kept his paws in country's waters—never more so than when he recorded at Muscle Shoals. As Williams told *Nashville Scene* in 1998, "Commencing in 1970, I sung about sex, niggers, love, rednecks, war, peace, dead flies, home wreckers, Sly Stone, my daughters, politics, revolution and blood transfusions (just to name a few), and never got out of character."

Country musicians began to flock to him. In 1971, producer Billy Sherrill and singer Johnny Paycheck covered Williams' "She's All I Got" and scored a massive hit, earning a CMA award nomination in the process. As Hughes points out, "the same year that Swamp Dogg released an album featuring the soul song 'Call Me Nigger,' Jerry Williams was honored as country songwriter of the year by BMI." Naturally, a white secretary "forgot" to send him an invitation to the awards dinner. Not that he was mad: "Most of the things that happened to me as a black man, I think was [sic] funny."

You can't help but smile to hear "I'll Take You There." Its exquisite craft sounds as elemental as water, earth, and air. Even a few seconds of the song's lyrical optimism is enough to turn up your lips. On that Sunday football advertisement in the nightclub it takes just about that long before the white male announcer tells us over scenes of credit cards being swiped and musical instruments and energy drinks being bought on the black ladies' "tour" that "the four old fine friends were once again the Five Fine Fillies. Before earning 1 percent cash back on all purchases, and 2 percent back on groceries, even before automatically earning 3 percent back on gas, Red Meg got a Bank America Cash Rewards credit card and called Little Lily to say 'It's time to rock.'" Perhaps, like me, before the ad was even halfway finished you realized with a twinge of cynicism that the auspiciousness of selling trumps all other political projects. Ceaselessly broken down into percentage points and rewards, it has always been the bottom line. In America, the time to sell is always now. Long before Dr. Martin Luther King, Jr.'s assassination and the Nixon/Reagan backlash began to overwhelm the Civil Rights era, its story of struggle has been one largely received in the lens of white expectation and broadcast by a media overwhelmed by white representation, built largely to put money in white pockets. *Country Soul* is an excellent place to begin a more honest accounting of this golden era.

Angela Bofill

Angel of the Night (1979)

As far as albums from 1979 go, Angela Bofill's *Angel of the Night* might not have been as immediately arresting as Michael Jackson's *Off The Wall* or Fleetwood Mac's *Tusk*, but it is certainly a more pleasurable listening experience than Pink Floyd's *The Wall* or The Clash's *London Calling*. Needless to say, Pink Floyd and The Clash's lurid fantasies of British fascism still sell by the ton, and Angela is dimly remembered by fifty-something R&B radio listeners who last bought a CD in 1996. Angela's legacy is also tarnished somewhat by a string of sometimes generic '80s electro-soul albums that were only saved by the fact that one of the finest and most talented Latin-American singers of the twentieth century was singing on them. The neon spray paint world of the '80s could be hard on brilliant and idiosyncratic jazz-pop artists of the 1970s.

To truly understand the breadth of Angela's talents, one must look to the two albums she made in the late '70s for Bob Grusin's GRP label. Her debut, 1978's *Angie*, finds Angela reaching the highest of bird song heights *a la* Flora Purim on her majestic, self-penned "Under The Moon And Over The Sky," and also reaching down deep for almost Robeson-esque African American art song gravity on an album that swells with vocal invention and cosmic soul import. Her universal pleas for the children of the world sung in that dark plum pudding (or flan soaked in rum) of a voice might have inadvertently invented the UNICEF-pop that Whitney drilled into our souls.

Her follow-up, 1979's *Angel of the Night*, is her masterpiece. There is nothing her voice can't do. Angela's magic comes from a higher place of mind and soul. She is *above* the dance floor, but not in a snooty way. She's too nice to gloat. And in keeping with the times, the title track's angel lyrically resembles Stevie Nicks more than any Christian deity. The album's opener, "I Try," written by Angela, is a better song than anything ever written by Roger Waters or Joe Strummer. It's also one of the finest songs of the decade. It aches and breaks so exquisitely, and it might make you want to be sad for a living. It's a stroke of genius.

In some ways, this album marked the end of an era—a hopeful and unselfconscious blend of Latin-inflected jazz/soul pop (that might strike some modern listeners as a little naïve in a Disney / Broadway way) made with real money by studio pros at the top of their game. The 1980s would be a different game altogether, a much less hopeful one. The last track on the album, "The Voyage," also self-penned, is an epic tribal call for peace that finds us sailing on a ship to a new galaxy of existence. With the grinning skulls of Reaganomics, crack, AIDS, and rainbow scrunchies just around the corner, this would be the last time in American pop music history that someone would ask us to see the world through a seagull's eyes. Which is really kind of a shame.

Jockmouth: the Sweatstival!

by JEFF JOHNSON & DAVID ROTH

5 STAGES OF SPORTS AND MUSIC ACROSS WISCONSIN'S HISTORIC ALPINE VALLEY CONCERT VENUE!

For three days in July, fans of sports and music will converge at the first annual Jockmouth Festival. In addition to live performances, fans will be treated to interactive events that bring them closer to the sports radio experience than they ever dreamed possible.

This doesn't just mean watching a 265-pound man in a pullover dourly rank the top fifteen quarterbacks in San Diego Chargers history. Imagine getting waterboarded by nacho cheese in the food tent while Mike Golic stifles a burp nearby. Or taking multiple "selfies" with attractive babes in t-shirts with the 5-Hour Energy logo on it—real women who will not be outwardly disapproving about your insistence on wearing Cincinnati Bengals overalls to special occasions. Spend up to 12 hours learning about the bold new look of Chrysler in the Gloat Zone, rubbing elbows with other famous sports radio callers, and being no closer than twenty-five yards and a six-man security detail from WFAN's Mike Francesa. Jockmouth is where it all comes together—a celebration of all the glorious sights, sounds, and smells of sports radio culture, except also there are a few women there.

THREE MUSKETEERS WATER™ STAGE

Three Musketeers Water™, a cloud of chocolatey liquid refreshment made with 100% natural nougat, is perfect for staying cool, hydrated, and hypoglycemic at the summer's hottest festivals.

FEATURING "JUST BOBBIN"

Bob Costas in conversation with the Grateful Dead's Bob Weir. Join Mr. Costas as he trawls tediously for sentiment and threads of old baseball mythology in the music of the Grateful Dead, with a long-winded and excruciatingly detailed digression about how Red Schoendienst preferred to store his luggage on the locomotives that took his ball clubs across the country, while Mr. Weir waits patiently. Because of Mr. Costas' aversion to live music, none will be played.

REMEMBER:

DETAILS ON PAGE 29!

AUTOTRADER.COM "HAS MY LIFE COME TO THIS?" STAGE

The number one online marketplace for people looking to buy, sell, or trade-in their cars is proud to present a stage dedicated to live performances by the biggest, brightest, and loudest voices in sports talk radio.

FEATURING MADCAP & THE WIMP
PERFORMING GREATEST MOMENTS FROM
"2001 ARIZONA DIAMONDBACKS SEASON"

Phoenix's dynamic duo has spent nearly seventeen years of AM drive-time accusing NFL quarterbacks of being gay and wishing bladder cancer on referees and umpires on KFCE 930, The Sportsface. In this live setting, they'll recall the hilarious summer of 2001, when they encouraged callers to try to dose Diamondbacks infielder Craig Counsell's newborn child with LSD.

FEATURING SQUELCHER & GURGLES SPORTSZONE

The reunion that no one believed was possible. This popular sports-talk duo would later drift apart due to creative differences—Squelcher is still on the air at Boston's WEEI, where he co-hosts "The Inconsolable Sports Dads" with longtime sidekick Racist Mike; Gurgles, now Shakti Dreamcatcher, lives near Sun Valley, Idaho, and is no longer involved with radio. A generous donation by Autotrader.com to Dreamcatcher's "Crystals For Kids" charity brought him out of retirement for one night only. The two will perform the classic 1994 routine in which they kidnapped former New England Patriots receiver Irving Fryar and held him captive for more than three weeks in a concrete basement in Lynn, Massachusetts. The legendary stunt earned the two a weeklong suspension from WEEI and thirty months in prison.

FEATURING DENNIS
ON THE CARPHONE

One of the most prolific and accomplished sports radio callers of his era, Dennis "On The Car Phone" Gelardi is a divorced father of four from Long Island's Nassau County who formerly worked in the wholesale deli meat business. His performance at Jockmouth will consist of him screaming about the New York Islanders for three hours and fifteen minutes.

LEE JEANS "TIME WARP" STAGE

FEATURING CRYSTAL CASTLES' TRIBUTE TO THE BUFFALO BILLS

Original members of the experimental Toronto-based band reunite to perform their little-heard song suite "Talley." Long a live favorite for the band, the song cycle—inspired by the Buffalo Bills of the late 1980's and named after long-tenured linebacker Darryl Talley—was never recorded due to a copyright dispute involving the band's use of unauthorized samples from longtime Bills NT Fred Smerlas' answering machine message. Recent acrimony within the band made it unlikely that "Talley" would ever be performed again, but an intervention by former Buffalo quarterback Frank Reich helped the feuding Alice Glass and Ethan Kath see past their differences. "Despite everything," Kath told Don Beebe of Buffalo Sports Radio's "Beebe And The Gunt" show, "we'll always love Frank Reich and sincerely want him to be happy."

1981-1982 INDIANA PACERS PERFORMING THE EAGLES' "HOTEL CALIFORNIA"

You might find yourself asking, "Is that Don Buse or Don Henley?" Though none of the 1981-1982 Indiana Pacers knew how to play an instrument, they didn't let that keep them from learning to play "Ho-tel California" on found objects in Holiday Inns amidst an otherwise forgettable season. More than three decades later, (most of) the team re-assembles for the first time to perform, participate in a Q&A led by Mitch Albom, and get served with a lawsuit by Henley himself.

1984 DETROIT TIGERS PERFORMING "ANGIE" BY THE ROLLING STONES

This is the only song they know, so fans will want to arrive promptly for what promises to be a short set. They do it really well. Kind of bossa nova via Hawaii. Darrell Evans actually sat in with a lot of bands when they came through the area back then, and Lou Whitaker sang backing vocals on a couple of Toto songs.

FORMER NFL PUNTER BRYAN BARKER'S DJ SCHOOL WITH ANIMAL COLLECTIVE

In the mid-2000s, Bryan Barker quit the game he loved to devote more time to following Animal Collective around. And also because he was forty-one. Watch Panda Bear and Deakin teach Bryan to DJ!

PEPCID AC TENT

Step into the Pepcid AC Mist tent—and try the new Pepcid AC inhaler, an innovative new way of administering a time-tested favorite.

FEATURING "THE CASE AGAINST JOHN WALL" BY COLIN COWHERD

Over five years ago, Washington Wizards point guard John Wall attempted to Dougie as an NBA rookie during his team's opening-night introduction. While other commentators steadfastly refused to give a shit, Colin Cowherd really, really did, and has never forgiven Wall for the shame this cowardly act brought to the game. Mr. Cowherd will serve as prosecutor in this live radio event from the Pepcid AC stage; Wale serves as defense attorney. Fans will fill out a card reading "When John Wall did the dance, I felt_____. How am I supposed to explain that to my kids?" Prospective jurors will be selected to serve on the jury alongside foreman Donald Trump. Celebrity journalist George Will acts as judge. When the verdict comes in guilty, cake will be served.

CLIF BAR EXERTION ALLEY

There's no better place to learn to rock climb than at a three-day sports and music festival that has not provided the proper equipment, and where it is certain that you will look like a loser if you do or don't participate. After climbing, everyone is invited to try new Clif Bar Steaks.

EVERY TICKET COMES WITH A GIFT BAG, INCLUDING:

A personal message of courage, recorded by CBS's Jim Nantz, looping on a keychain courtesy of 16 Handles.

Microwavable Ben Gay torso wraps—when Ace Bandages aren't enough, zap a microwavable Ben Gay torso wrap and then weave it around whatever aches.

Keurig coffee pods, in new flavors like "Workplace Hangover," "3:45pm Again," and "Hot Paste."

A certificate for a free digital download of Steve Vai's "Introductions," in which the guitar virtuoso plays electrifying versions of twenty-five famous sports talk radio themes.

No Longer Can
I Remain Earthbound:
Future's Long, Strange
Trip from Pluto to
the Underworld

by MEAGHAN GARVEY

I feel great," Future wheezes from the far side of a squelchy leather couch in a London studio, former BBC DJ Tim Westwood perched at the other end. A giant oil rendering of Jimi Hendrix, Future's longtime idol ("Future Hendrix" was the original title for his sophomore album, before he abandoned the concept for *Honest*), looms above them, by uncanny coincidence. Westwood congratulates Future on the birth of Future Zahir Wilburn, his son with Ciara, now almost six months old; the two called off their engagement three months ago. The time since, if his post-breakup tracks are a reliable indicator, has been a nonstop bender. "Blessed, I feel blessed," he mutters, his voice barely registering above a croak. His usually radiant face is bloated and patchy with stubble, Versace shades never leaving his eyes. He looks like shit.

This moment is as close to a breaking point as the fiercely private rapper has shown off the mic, though he doesn't have time to melt down. It's November 2014, and for now, Future is riding high (or, rather, low) off the release of *Monster*: It is music unmistakably born from pain, careening recklessly from rage to numbness. It is the return of the old Future, rabid and snarling. "What is that whole 'monster' vibe that we are dealing with?" Westwood asks gingerly, sensing something is about to boil over. These will be the last words he says for the rest of the twenty-four minute interview, which has ceased to

be an interview and is now a stream-of-consciousness monologue, a spleen-letting. "The inner monster in me, you know?" Future sighs. "Everything that I went through, that shit just made me a monster. The hits, the fame, the money, the haters, the blogs, the negativity that goes along with being an entertainer." He describes the mounting guilt that he'd abandoned the sounds and values of where he came from—the notorious Kirkwood neighborhood of East Atlanta, nicknamed Lil' Mexico—for glossy, world-conquering ballads about looking for love with a flashlight.

As Future spills his guts—Westwood simply nodding from the other end of the couch—something strange starts to happen. He has always employed a rotating cast of alter-egos that help identify and express his moods: Future Hendrix, Super Future, Fire Marshall Future, the Astronaut Kid, and now, Monster. They serve as a shield, too: It's hard to get a solid read on someone constantly slipping between personas, compartmentalizing himself so thoroughly that it's almost impossible to see a whole. But as he speaks, Future's personas begin to weave in and out, entangling themselves in real time. He invokes Future Hendrix, Monster, and just plain Future in the same breath, lapsing in and out of his characters until they blur into a delirious, staggering hybrid, seemingly guided by Monster's manic id.

After twenty minutes uninterrupted, Future suddenly sits up straight. "This is me in the flesh right now. Tomorrow I might not look like this. It's just 'cause... I can do what the fuck I wanna do." He rambles a bit longer, and then suddenly he's done talking, and he gets up and walks out, cackling to himself. The Monster has left the building.

Future's fascination with outer space—both literal and metaphorical—is well documented. He sang ecstatically about lifting off toward the moon on the 2011 mixtape cut "Blast Off"; space was triumph, ascendence fueled by hustle. "I'm gone to the moon / I float like balloons," he crowed later that year on *Streetz Calling*, maybe the strongest project of his early mixtape days. Space was a beckoning black hole, a drug-fueled escape from reality. By early 2012, Future was so invested in his Astronaut Kid persona that he'd named his new mixtape *Astronaut Status*. But on *Pluto*, one of the best major label rap debuts of the past decade, space represented sheer limitlessness: it obliterated the distinction between rapping and singing, pop and street, with menace and romance and struggle and hope all coexisting.

That Future was particularly drawn to Pluto goes beyond space and into the rapper's strange parallels with the ex-planet's mythological namesake. The name Pluto first emerged from the Greek Plouton ("Giver of Wealth") as an alternate, yet characteristically distinct, representation of the god better known as Hades, ruler of the Underworld in classical mythology. Hades was the most fearsome of all the gods, to the point that people were afraid to even speak his name out loud; Plouton emerged as a euphemistic stand-in somewhere around the fifth century BC. But though they share origin myths and preside over the same subterranean dominion, Pluto and Hades are neither the same god nor fully distinct entities. As with Future and his rotating cast of alter-egos, perhaps the easiest way to understand them is as two divergent personalities within one being at the same damn time.

One of six children of the Titans Cronus and Rhea, Hades and his brothers Zeus and Poseidon overthrew their father and divided his worldly kingdom into three separate realms: sea, sky, and the dark Underworld. And so Hades descended into the earth's core, where he would guard the souls of the dead ad infinitum. Cruel, pitiless, and forbidding, Hades as a character never quite emerges from the dark and inescap-able realm of Hades the place. Violence is embedded into his identity: it is the driving force behind his best-known myth, the abduction of Persephone, his unwilling future wife and a perennial prisoner of the Underworld. He was drawn by a chariot pulled by four pitch-black horses and accompanied by a vicious three-headed dog, Cerebus. But Pluto represents a less fearsome side of the god, and with it, a relatively optimistic view of the afterlife as a concept—one that presented death and rebirth in harmony.

In his dialogue *Cratylus*, Plato presented the corporeal self as an impediment to virtue, weighed down by the bodily desires and inherent evils of human nature. As such, he argued, death is liberation: "For I affirm with the greatest seriousness that the union of the soul with this terrestrial body is never better than the separation of them." In this sense, Pluto represents neither the concept of Hell as damnation, nor even death itself. Instead, he is a god of dissolution, of the separation of body and soul—not as a dreaded end, but as a clean slate. In his own dependence on shifting personas, dissolution is a concept with which Future is well-acquainted. But where his inner Hades and Pluto were once distinguishable, the Westwood interview, along with his recent mixtape work, suggests that the characters have become inextricably tangled: a dissociative identity crisis that has bled into his non-musical life.

Before Monster, Future Hendrix, the Astronaut Kid, or even regular old Future, there was Nayvadius Wilburn (he'd later legally change it to Nayvadius Cash), born in 1983 and raised in East Atlanta. His older cousin was Rico Wade, founding member of production team Organized Noize and in whose basement studio the Dungeon Family would take shape—a collective that, like Future would go on to do, made approachably strange and distinctively Southern popular music without pandering to the radio or abandoning the hood. Back then, Future rapped as Meathead and wrote as part of the Organized Noize songwriting team. When he wasn't in the studio, he was hustling in Lil' Mexico, a life that would inform his prolific mixtape run from 2010 to 2012.

He hit the Billboard Top 50 in 2011 with "Racks"—technically a YC song, but for all practical purposes, a Future song—and followed up with a ridiculous solo single, "Tony Montana." His voice was spellbinding, almost paradoxical: sometimes it

It's a scene straight out of Homer's
description of Hades' terrain in the Odyssey:
a stark, windless field covered in Pluto's beloved
narcissus flowers known as the Asphodel Meadows,
the part of the Underworld where the souls of average
men—not good, not evil—will roam in perpetuity.

was hoarse and ragged, sometimes smooth and melodic; when it cracked it sounded like his heart was breaking. He used Autotune not as a corrective, but to accentuate his voice's flaws; like T-Pain and Lil Wayne in their respective primes, the effect only emphasized the humanity and emotion behind it. At Pluto's release party, Atlanta's most influential rappers of the 2000s—Jeezy, Gucci, T.I., Big Boi—paid their respects, confirmation that legendary spoken word poet Big Rube wasn't exaggerating on the album's intro: "No longer can I remain earthbound. The future is now."

Post-*Pluto*, Future indulged his inner romantic, giddily following where it led. On "Real and True," he watched his extraterrestrial soulmate, played by one Miley Cyrus, fade into the distance as his spacecraft takes off: "Through the distant and cold depths of space / The radio sings our song / It's a love real and true." But it was Ciara's spring 2013 single "Body Party" that felt most like a turning point: an ode to her and Future's still-new love, his infatuated coos her background vocals. The video playfully mythologized the couple's introduction—eyes meet across the dancefloor, a shy conversation in the Grecian peristyle, love at first sight.

It was during this period that Future developed another alter ego: Future Hendrix, a persona that took full form in the lean-soaked, heart-on-sleeve street ballads he pumped out during the first half of 2013. Of Future's many personas, Hendrix seemed the closest to his heart—if not his truest self, certainly his best. "[Future Hendrix] is freedom and passion, freedom of

expression," he told *SPIN* in 2013. "Just being myself." Future Hendrix was a diehard romantic, and Ciara fit perfectly into his life as both a partner and a muse. But Future Hendrix was also impulsive and moody and restless. And besides that, the streets didn't want Future Hendrix. They wanted the old Future, that Dirty Sprite, Lil' Mexico–bred Future. That Future reemerged as Fire Marshall Future (named for the frequency with which fire marshalls shut down his raucous, sold-out 2013 shows) on "Karate Chop" and "Sh!t": street singles bellowed in raspy staccato that dramatically redirected the course of his sophomore album from "Future Hendrix" to *Honest*.

With the Shakespearean romance of Pluto setting a precedent—not to mention that Future and Ciara were officially engaged, Ciara pregnant and glowing—many expected *Honest* to be an album rife with bliss. But, as Future stressed to *Pitchfork* in 2014: "There are no love songs on this album." With an identity crisis in full swing, it stands to reason that he had begun to view "love songs" as "pop songs," the antithesis of the gritty realism that shaped his mixtape work. To wit: "I Won"—a Kanye West collaboration presented as *Honest*'s "for the ladiez" single—feels cold and hollow, reducing the bachelors' respective fiancées to symbols of their own excellence. However, the album's tender "I Be U" complicates Future's assessment of the record, and it instantly became his most poignant love song to date.

"Thinking how you would be thinking, I'm holding you close," he sings in an uncharacteristically hushed tone. "I'm dreaming how you would be dreaming." It's no coincidence that the song

is a thousand times more moving than the album's similarly ti-
tled ballad, "I'll Be Yours." Given his reliance on multiple personalities to make sense of his own head, it follows that Future's
most affecting love song comes from not just loving his partner,
but becoming her: their corporeal selves become irrelevant, the
physical separation between them dissolves, and their souls
fuse. "Your spirit, my spirit illuminates through our bodies / I
feel we whole," he sings. By becoming his partner, he's reached
a new understanding of his own identity, and for a rare moment,
it appears he is at peace.

Pluto's reluctant bride, Persephone, is sometimes known as
Kore, an almost callously reductive name that simply translates
to "maiden," or "girl." The daughter of harvest goddess Demeter and Pluto's brother Zeus (incest wasn't particularly frowned
upon within the Greek pantheon), she is also the personification
of the earth's abundant vegetation. She was picking flowers in a
field with her nymph girlfriends when Pluto—in some tellings of
the abduction myth, having been struck by Cupid's love arrow—
bursts through the Earth's surface on his horse-drawn chariot like
some mythological Kool-Aid Man and drags her, screaming, into
Hades. Demeter threatens to curse the earth with famine until her
daughter is returned, leaving mankind in peril. Pluto promises to
release her, but first, in a calculated move, he feeds her pomegran-
ate seeds; having tasted the food of the Underworld, she is bound
to spend one season per year in his subterranean realm for eternity. This barren part of the year, during which Persephone serves
as the Underworld's harsh and majestic queen, is understood as
winter; her return to earth signifies spring.

Though there is extensive documentation of Persephone's affect
on the earth once she leaves her subterranean prison, there is
seemingly very little that details the seasons of the year during
which Pluto exists in Hades alone. It's easy to imagine, though,
that it's something akin to what Future depicts on Monster: a
thrashing, seething, intoxicated, knee-jerk response to heartbreak, in which the monster-god blames himself. The tape is a
red-eyed blur of xans, percs, molly, lean and forgettable sex, but
its emotional crux is comprised of three crucial songs that stand
as some of Future's best and most candid work. "Throw Away"
is his breaking point, the first crack in the Monster's armor.
"Girl, you know you like a pistol, you a throwaway," he growls,
Monster fully in control. But halfway through, the beat changes, and out of nowhere, he invokes Future Hendrix. Instantly his

defenses crumble, his heart bleeds through, and he cries out to
the howling void where his partner used to be: "Do you feel better by yourself? Did you feel better when I left?"

"Hardly," another Future Hendrix–style ballad, confirms something Future has hinted at for years: as much as he attempts to
dull his pain through substance abuse, his memory is mercilessly-
ly pristine. "Hardly, hardly, hardly, hardly forget anything," he
whimpers on its hook, leaving no doubt he means it as a curse.
The song is dedicated to the memory of his friend, OG Double D,
a longtime affiliate of Future's Freebandz label. Seemingly minor memories bubble to the surface, like the chinchilla fur D was
wearing in the studio when Future recorded "Chosen One." "I'm
easily agitated, get intoxicated trying to fight the demons," he
croaks. Retreating deeper into his own pounding head—much
like Pluto, alone but for the dead—memories are his sole, unin-
vited companions. Pluto knew the respite of drugs, too; the God
of the Undead wore wreaths of intoxicating phasganion and narcissus flowers, known for their narcotic drugginess, erotic fascination, and imminent death. To dream of crowning oneself with
narcissus was said to be a bad omen, a reckless romanticization
of death, not unlike Future's obsession with the myth of Hendrix's drug-fuelled creativity.

Monster's heaviest blow is its closing track, "Codeine Crazy,"
a desperate arm emerging from beneath a roiling purple sea.
"Drownin' in Actavis / suicide," he warbles, too high to raise his
voice much above a murmur but still not high enough to numb
the pain entirely. In the video, Future finds himself alone but
for his double styrofoam in a barren, purple-tinged field; it's
late fall on the precipice of winter, almost time for Persephone
to descend into the Earth's shadowy core. It's a scene straight
out of Homer's description of Hades' terrain in the *Odyssey*: a
stark, windless field covered in Pluto's beloved narcissus flowers
known as the Asphodel Meadows, the part of the Underworld
where the souls of average men—not good, not evil—will roam
in perpetuity. Future awakes to a vision of a woman in all white
with glowing purple eyes; it seems unlikely that she is more than
a mirage. Still, he staggers up, double cup in hand, and blindly
stumbles after her. It's Persephone's abduction myth reversed
into a submissive, desperate fantasy: he is powerless against
her this time, as she lures him toward the earthly realm from
which she manifested. Staggering through the Asphodel Meadows, Future—or is it Pluto, or Hades, or Monster?—relinquishes
control, losing himself to the sweet, crushing certainty of fate.
Four horses gallop across the meadow—Pluto's chariot-leaders,
finally free. At the end of the video, the woman in white is gone,
and he is alone.

What Happens When There Are No Boys in the Room

A Q&A with Robyn

by LAURA SNAPES
Photo by Erik Sanchez

There's scarcely a quiet corner in the student union building of KTH, Stockholm's Royal Institute of Technology. There's the warm chemical squeak of 3-D printers shaping diodes for light-up necklaces, the unadulterated noise of 200 curious teenage girls discovering virtual reality—or, rather, figuring out how to hack their own. As load-bearing robots crash into one another a few meters away, Robyn finds comparative peace on a couch and takes a moment to contemplate what she's created. This is Tekla, the inaugural one-day teen-girl tech fest that she's put together with KTH and her publicist Lina Thomsgard, with support from Google, Spotify, and a few other tech companies.

In September 2013, KTH awarded Robyn their Great Prize, which recognizes scientific ingenuity and a unique artist who "exerts a powerful influence particularly on the spiritual life of her own people." Giving a talk to the students at KTH is a condition of acceptance, but Robyn, having read about the low uptake of STEM courses among young women, wanted to create something for the potential next generation of students. The vision for Tekla was downright utopian: the eleven-to-eighteen-year-olds here were carefully selected with racial and economic diversity in mind, and the day's various workshops offer crash-courses in the likes of music production, API creation, hacking, and online security. It was initially planned as a one-off, but halfway through the day, Robyn and Lina are already talking about making it an international event, or sharing the template so that others might start similar festivals, with the addition of an international pop star optional.

I sat down with Robyn to discuss her own relationship with technology, the gendering of success, and why she likes to work solo.

When you were a young girl, did you have any gateway to technology?

No, not at all. I had a gateway for other things. My parents used to have a theater group and they were on stage a lot, so that became [normal] for me. When you develop an interest, it usually comes from [being in] an environment where you're able to find your own entrance into it. I think if I had been exposed to technology or mathematics, it could have just as well been that, and that's what Tekla is about, that there is this playful and relaxed space where you're able to develop an interest. Guys form a band and they sit around with their guitars, or they do a sport together or whatever—I think boys already have it in them that they're allowed to try, and make a mistake, and then try again.

Men get to fail.

The boy circle allows failure. Boys are tough on each other as well, but there's at least this thing of, like, you're not expected to not be able to do it. You know that thing when you're in school and you do sports and you're chosen to a team and then it's like, Oh no, we don't want a girl! You hear that all the time when you're a girl. We're rarely in a girl group where we allow each other to just play around and try stuff.

Lina said you had questioned whether it was the right thing to do to exclude boys, because girls will have to interact with them when they get out into the wider world. But ultimately it was about creating that space.

Yeah, and to see what happens when there are no boys in the room. Maybe a girl decides that she wants to play the drums, and she wouldn't if there was a boy there. A different dynamic happens.

When girls get to a certain age, they become uncertain about themselves and conceal parts of their identity, but the Internet has opened up these spaces for girls to express their identities.

At a certain age you start to look at yourself differently and become aware of who you're supposed to be in relation to other people, and for me, that structure is everywhere. It's in school, it's in your family, and it's impossible to get away from. Isolating in a group is really important, but then of course the next stage has to be to create the kind of awareness that you can bring back into your environment where that stuff happens. You're able to dip into other worlds that connect to what you're doing as well without having to be a part of that overall structure, because it's the overall structure that really kills it. You access the information and you can use it in your own way.

I know of so many private communities online for female creatives, and they're so empowering and constructive. Is it true that there's a Listserv just for all the female musicians in Sweden?

A Swedish female musician started it, and it's a big network now and I'm a part of it. You can post questions or thoughts or requests—like if you want to find a female saxophone player or whatever—but also there's a lot of discussions about problems we all encounter; you can talk about things that might not be as easy to talk about in another environment. It's very empowering.

How has technology empowered you? When did you start involving yourself in taking the reigns of the means of production?

It happened quite early. I always used music programs and have always edited my own vocals, and early on I started to work with Logic. But it's not until maybe four years ago that I've actually started to produce on my own. It wasn't natural until I decided to do it [and started hanging out] with friends of mine like Zhala, who do it already.

So finding female community has been really important to you.

Very, very important. Because, again, it de-dramatizes things, like you're able to connect it to your own work, a real aspect of your life,

not this image of what boys do when they do that thing. You bring it down to a level where you're able to grasp it in a different way.

Has technology liberated your self-image or self-conception?

Totally. It can be simple things, like if I know how to bounce certain channels in Logic, [laughs] zip it up and mail it to a musician that I'm working with. That discussion [that follows] happens in a different way than if a male producer I work with sent them to someone. That I'm the author of that email, that it's just me, I'm doing it on my own, creates a different discussion about what it is that I've recorded, because I recorded it on my own.

You don't have those filters of being translated by other people.

Exactly. Technology keeps your integrity intact.

Is that what you aim to do, to create as independently as you can?

I like to collaborate, so I don't see that I have to be making music totally on my own in the future. But, when I do, something else happens: I get a better picture of who I am as a musician. Certain things come out of it that wouldn't have happened otherwise. When you work with someone else and they're supposed to produce your songs, you're always trying to guess what the other person is looking for, and there's always a disconnect in the way you interpret the other person. With something that I've done totally on my own, the nuances become so much more, and it's easier to communicate, it's easier to be precise. So that's my goal: be more precise about where it is I want to go. And then getting there is also interesting, together with another person.

Because I'm not an experienced beat-programmer [laughs a little], I tend to make beats that are a little bit off, and I think it's a good thing—that's what people seem to like about them. There are things I really like about drum sounds, for example, that I'm now starting to realize how I actually get there. But on the way to getting there, I also realize what it is that I can't do [laughs]. And those things that are not really working, they create possibilities too.

Is that a way you've always worked? Being open to the idea of mistakes?

Because I'm self-taught, I always have to trust my instincts. Being able to trust my ear, what it is that I'm hearing, [believing] that there's an intelligence in what I'm hearing even if I can't explain it,

Yeah, and to see what happens when there are no boys in the room. Maybe a girl decides that she wants to play the drums, and she wouldn't if there was a boy there.

and then find the language for how to explain it—that's kind of my process. That's what it's been so far, and now I'm trying to actually learn what it is that I'm doing, but without losing my ear, my own way of hearing it.

Last year, when you were working and touring with Royksopp, there was still that perception that they were making the beats and you were just the singer. What do you think makes it so inconceivable that women could be doing these things?

Because we're not portrayed doing it. I think that's why that campaign of women photographing themselves in front of mixers and computers that Björk started was really good. It's again about this group thing. We don't have the natural instinct to isolate in groups, not the way boys do.

Why do you think that is?

I think it's because we're biologically programmed to have babies earlier, as simple as that. We're programmed to take the responsibility for that, and it makes us, at a certain age, stop [being] interested in ourselves. We focus on boys or we focus on the way we look. I think it's really that simple. We stop looking inward.

One of the popular narratives about young girls and technology at the moment is that a) they're obsessed with self-image, and b) the Internet is warping that horribly for them. That narrative is always negative. It cuts out the idea that radical vanity can also be liberating—they're editing and shaping their own identity on their own terms.

I totally agree, and it's really important to question it: How do we look at ourselves through the Internet? There are certain things that I think we're gonna look back at and realize that they were totally unnecessary or totally weird, about how we decided to portray ourselves on the Internet. We're a little bit like kids, all children on the Internet: nobody really knows how it's going to affect our lives. Maybe people will hate me for saying this, but I think it's important to be critical of [how] girls feel that they have to expose themselves on the Internet. I know I sound like a fucking dry moralist, but there is a difference between taking a selfie in front of a computer [and] taking a selfie in front of the mirror. For boys as well. The Internet excludes so much content. It reproduces images you've seen a thousand times before, and sometimes our ability to decode pictures is not as advanced as the technology. We send out these signals all the time, but we really don't understand.

Has the Internet changed the way you see yourself?

Yes. In the beginning, it really gave me a tool to look at myself and analyze myself. And it's easy to become self-critical in that way. But it's also been a tool to shave off layers.

How do you mean?

Watching myself on the Internet or on TV made me realize how much I hide myself, too.

How do you hide yourself?

With body language, or by putting on clothes that create an armor. It made me more interested in soft aspects of my personality.

Have you pushed past that?

Maybe I haven't really been able to do it all the way yet, maybe that's what I'm trying to do for the next time I'm really visible in the media. Right now my way of handling it is being very careful with myself, careful with how much I'm in pictures—it's a very intuitive kind of need that I have at the moment, that I'm realizing my vulnerability.

You had a whole pop career before the Internet was really a thing, but then it worked to your benefit when you came back on your own terms. Do you feel lucky for not having grown up with that? Or do you wish you had had these tools?

I'm lucky to have been around in the transition. It's nice to have the before and after. The people who are our age at the moment, there is a sense of the time before, when you didn't have all that. I'm very into the idea of slowing down at the moment, and slowing the speed of information down as well. There's so much access to everything, and that's great, but I really want to be able to decide what it is that I'm taking in, and how much, because there's something that happens in the space between things that just can't happen when you're exposed to impressions all the time.

That space to percolate information.

I feel like an old lady saying these things! But I think that's gonna be probably the lesson for all of us—not just on a personal level; I'm saying as a society as a whole. We're breaking things apart so much, I don't know if it's healthy. I don't know if the amount of impressions we have on us all the time now allows for that way of turning information around, because it pacifies you, it numbs you. You're never able to process it and do something new with it.

A lot of the narrative about young women pushed by women's media is that they're always in competition with one another. There's something gently radical about bringing them together and creating community.

Yes, and it's on a very basic level, you know, because all girls won't like each other, and all boys don't like each other. But to just make it more normal, instead of either "girl power!" or "catfight!" Can we just talk about it in a different way, please? It gets tiring when it has to be that extreme.

Feminism has to be for all girls, the radical punk girls but also the girls with fake tans who go clubbing.

Yeah, totally, exactly, and that's where the slut-shaming comes in. I think it's important to be soft. To be—really, to be careful. Maybe that's what it is.

With the way you portray yourself?

With how much we give out.

Women are expected to give a lot of themselves anyway.

Exactly. ✐

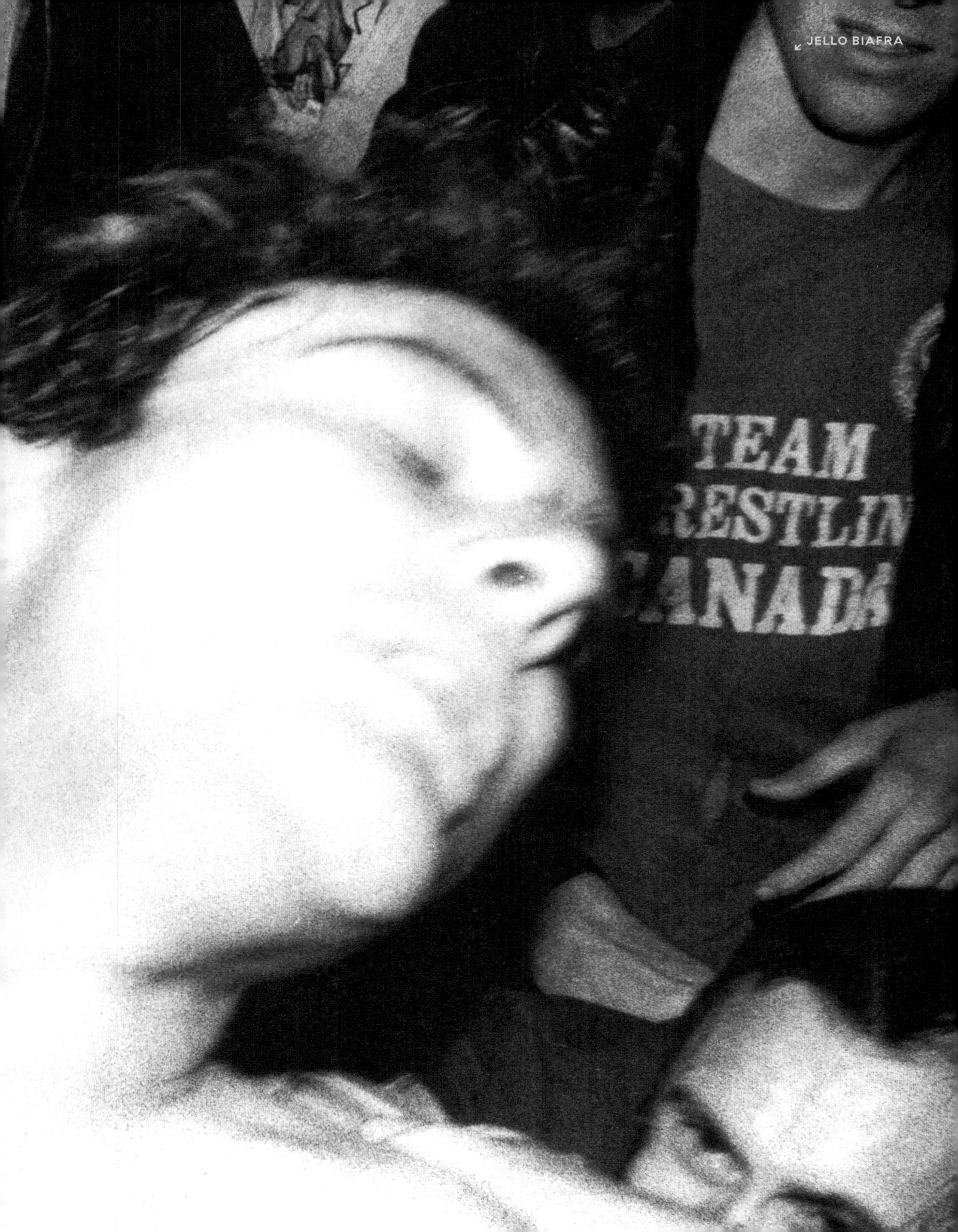

↙ JELLO BIAFRA

Paradise Lost

John Roberts' Rediscovered Photographs Capture the DIY San Francisco Scene of 1979–80

TEXT BY JOSEPH BIEN-KAHN
PHOTOS BY JOHN ROBERTS

↓

"The scene at the time—everybody had a band, it didn't matter if you were capable of anything. If you wanted to function socially, you put together a band, and you'd go play."

J.C. GARRETT LEAD SINGER OF THE ALTERBOYS AND CO-FOUNDER OF CLUB FOOT

By the time Joan Didion published her essay "Slouching Towards Bethlehem" in 1967, she could sense the shine beginning to fade off the Summer of Love. There was supposed to be a monumental shift—young people taking control, a true sea change in stale old Capitalist America. But (as it has a way of doing) the center did hold and by the 1970s even San Francisco was overrun by stadium shows, Cock Rock, and a loss of innocence.

Late in the decade, a darkness had begun to move in. Jim Jones moved his People's Temple from San Francisco down to the Caribbean Coast of South America. On November 18, 1978, following increased scrutiny, charges of human rights violations, and the killing of a United States congressman, Jones led a "revolutionary suicide" in which 913 members drank lethal doses of cyanide-laced Kool-Aid. Less than two weeks later, recently resigned city supervisor Dan White assassinated Mayor George Moscone and gay-rights activist Harvey Milk.

Amid this grim cultural moment punk rock came to San Francisco. As J.C. Garrett, lead singer of the Alterboys and co-founder of the art punk venue Club Foot, remembers, "I always refer to the summer of '77 as the Summer of Loathe because people were fed up with the phony love stuff." According to Steve Wascovich, founder of the Superior Viaduct label and self-proclaimed "lay person punk archivist," in 1977 Dirk Dirksen's Mabuhay Gardens was the only venue to play punk music in the city. However, by the time the Sex Pistols played their final show at Winterland Ballroom in January 1978, San Francisco's punk scene was viable, blooming. "Suddenly, you saw this explosion of venues that was happening," Wasovich said. "And in these kind of spaces, anything can happen.

This venue boom in '78 and '79 moved the scene from North Beach (where the tiny punk movement orbited around Dirksen's Mab) out to the Mission, the Tenderloin, and the Dogpatch, where artists lived. In these spaces bizarre was the norm. Many on stage and in the audience were San Francisco Art Institute students, who pushed the city's scene toward an original, absurdist style of punk. Today we think of punk as guitar, bass, and drums played fast and loud, but there was no such unifying sound in that early San Francisco scene. Tuxedo Moon was a violinist, a clarinetist, and a keyboardist who all wore slacks. Z'EV rhythmically hammered on a car bumper or banged a chain of milk cartons against the stage. One night at Club Foot—Garrett's DIY club out in Dogpatch— Glen Pape performed while wearing his bed.

In 1979, an art student at Hampshire College named John Roberts came west to study at the San Francisco Art Institute. He followed his art school friends to the different small clubs popping up around the city, and was quickly seduced by the two-minute bursts of energy and the originality of the scene. He brought his camera to every show, shooting while pogoing in the front row.

After struggling to make it professionally in New York in the early '80s, Roberts quit photography but continued to lug a suitcase of old prints and a shoebox of negatives with him each time he moved for the next three decades. Late in 2014, months before being moved to end-of-life care for renal cell cancer, Roberts told his son's friend Enosh Baker about the box of negatives. Baker enlisted local artist Sean Vranizan to help him scour nearly 13,000 negatives; the two began to convert their favorites to digital images. In March 2015, Roberts's work was finally shown at Chez Poulet in the San Francisco Mission District.

Roberts's pictures communicate the visceral energy of that early punk scene. They also capture something else entirely: the fact that the scene was small, a blip in the pre-AIDS and post-hippy San Francisco scene. The same faces keep showing up on stage and in the audience and they don't look anything like the faces on the streets around them. San Francisco was still full of aging flower children, tanned disco fans, and old white businessmen.

Soon after Roberts moved back to the East Coast, the diverse scene became more codified and more recognizably punk rock. Most of the early bands broke up, and others got managers and nursed dreams of making it. The strange, fertile underground scene scattered. The Offs expatriated to New York. Tuxedo Moon struck it big once they landed in Europe. The Avengers and the Pink Section broke up and became legends retrospectively. The devotees of the hardcore scene started to fill the clubs. Of that short art punk moment from '77 to the end of '79, only the Dead Kennedys made a lasting name outside San Francisco.

There was no distinctive sound to that early scene. There was no distinctive look. It was a bunch of art students and outcasts creating something in the void left when the San Francisco Sound vanished. Roberts was lucky enough to be there to capture it on film before it faded.

—Joseph Bien-Kahn, June 2015

THE BAY OF PIGS, (FROM LEFT TO RIGHT) ANDREW HAYES, JOSEPH JACOBS, & RICHARD KELLY

"There were people dressed in all different kinds of ways. There were graphic artists and fashion designers and photographers and punks and people who just wanted to get totally fucking wasted."

MATT HECKERT GUITARIST OF THE PINK SECTION

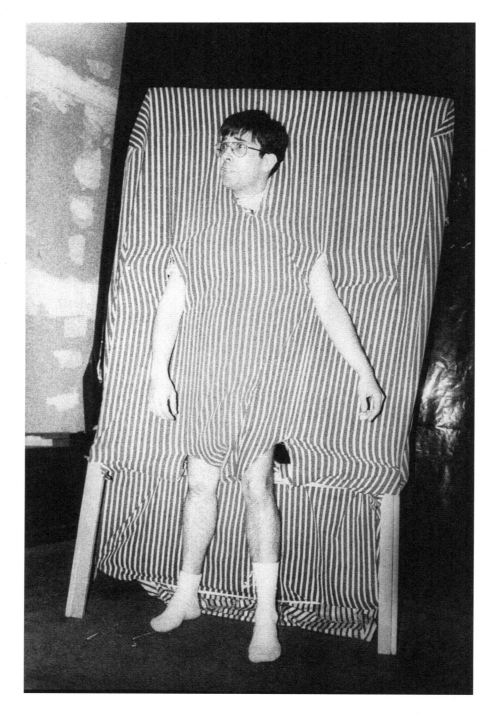

"We felt like we were doing our best to wash away the stale kind of cock-rock or
stadium-rock. We were taking a stand against how rock 'n' roll had turned into this
corporate thing that was not interesting at all and had nothing to do with young people.
And that we were just turning it back into true kernel of what it originally had been,
which was youthful rebellion against fucked-up society."

PENELOPE HOUSTON LEAD SINGER OF THE AVENGERS

← GLENN PAPE, IN 1980, STAGING A PERFORMANCE ART PIECE AT CLUB FOOT FROM THE INSIDE OF HIS BED. SELLIER WEBSTER (AKA SALLY MUTANT) AND SUE WHITE (AKA SUE MUTANT) WERE MEMBERS OF THE MUTANTS

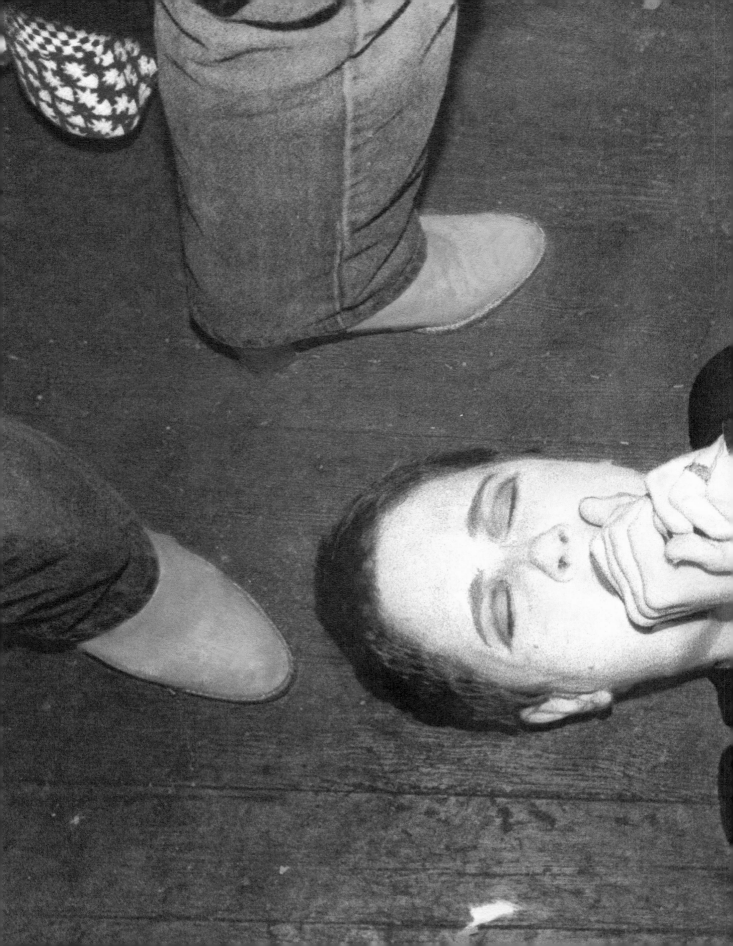

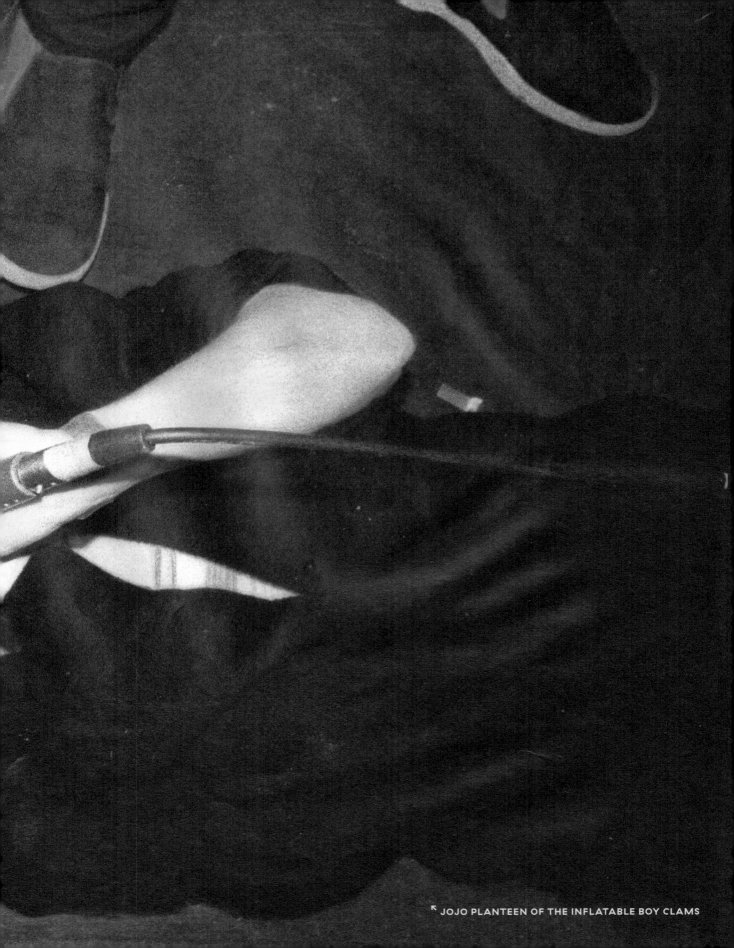

JOJO PLANTEEN OF THE INFLATABLE BOY CLAMS

TUXEDOMOON, (FROM LEFT TO RIGHT) BLAINE REININGER, STEVEN BROWN, AND PETER PRINCIPLE

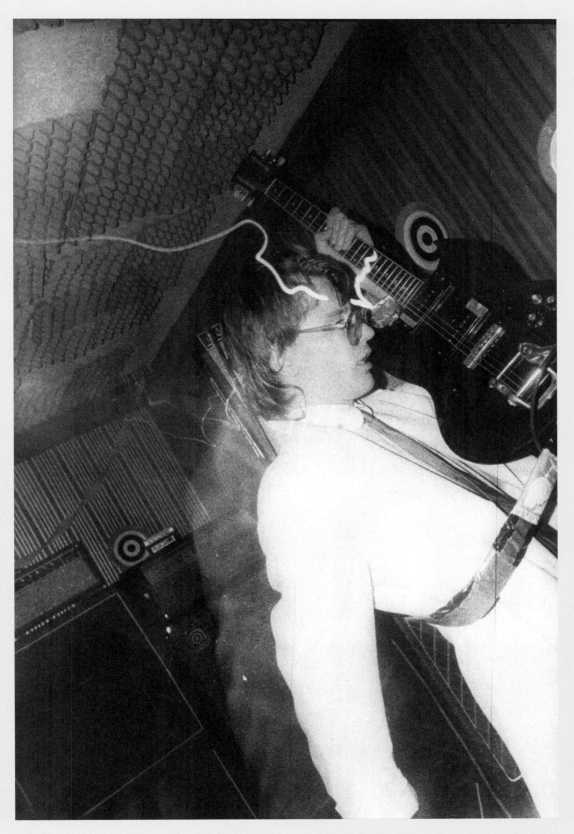

RICHARD KELLY, GUITARIST FROM THE ALTERBOYS, ALSO CO-FOUNDED CLUB FOOT WITH JC GARRETT.

"As Charles Hagen of the Mutants said at one point to me: There were no rules. The only rule was, you get up on stage and whatever you do, it can't be boring and it shouldn't be like what your friend just did."

STEVE WASCOVICH, FOUNDER OF SUPERIOR VIADUCT

"It was a grand time that was short–lived and I'm really happy that I was there. But I would never want to go through it again, in my wizened years, with what I know."

MATT HECKERT GUITARIST OF THE PINK SECTION

And now, an exclusive excerpt from Anders Nilsen's new book, *Poetry is Useless*, published by Drawn + Quarterly. Anders says: "It's a collection of comics, drawings, travelogue, memoir, political satire... and other weirder stuff pulled from my sketchbooks and my blog. Oh, and it has an index. Which is my favorite part."

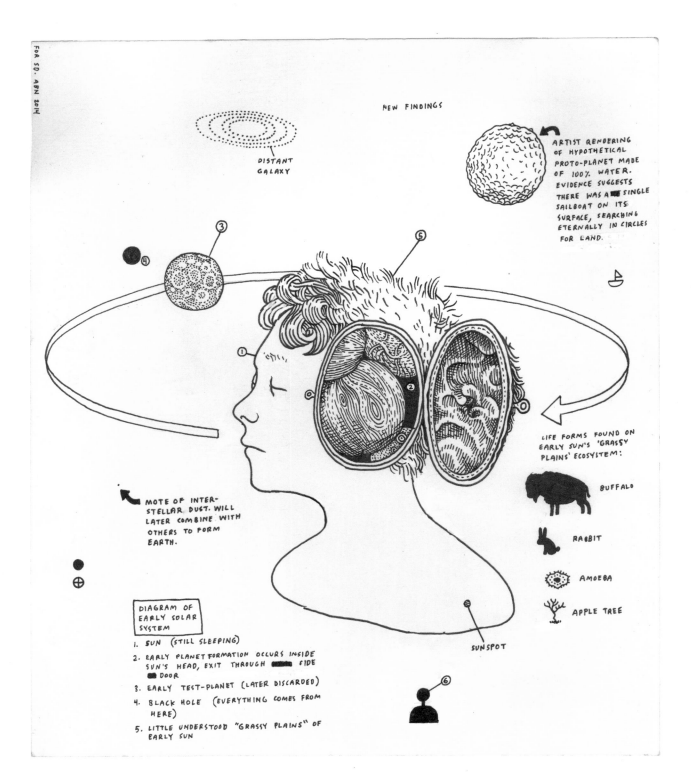

PITCHFORK *TOONS* • ANDERS NILSEN

True Myth

A Conversation with Sufjan Stevens

BY RYAN DOMBAL

Hanging from scaffolding on an in-progress luxury condo near Sufjan Stevens' office-slash-studio in Brooklyn, a huge sign promises to "preserve the history but change the meaning." The phrase is a euphemism for gentrification at its highest levels—an advertisement meant to appeal to the delirious grandeur of those willing and able to spend $5 million on an apartment. But in a different context, those same words can take on an odd profundity. When I relay the sign's message to Stevens, he lets out a little laugh. "That could be the title of my autobiography," he says.

For the last fifteen years, Stevens has mixed his own life history with fantastical images and stories of the ages—from the Bible, Greek mythology, American fables—inventing a new sort of twenty-first-century folklore along the way. But while this creative strategy has led to him being regarded as one of the finest songwriters on the planet, it's also taken a personal toll. "My imagination can be a problem," he says. "I'm prone to making my life, my family, and the world around me complicit in my cosmic fable, and often it's not fair to manipulate the hard facts of life into a vision quest. But it's all an attempt to extract meaning, and ultimately that's what I'm in pursuit of, like; what's the significance of these experiences?"

Named after his mother and stepfather, Stevens' seventh studio album *Carrie & Lowell* once again combines fact and fiction, though it finds the ambitious artist's more fanciful tendencies drastically pared-down. Musically, it's easily his most bare album, with most songs offering only crystalline acoustic guitar or piano along with Stevens' ghostly whisper of a singing voice. There are no orchestral crescendos, no electronic freakouts, no drums. Stevens jokingly describes the album's sound as "easy listening," though it's more akin to the harrowing moodiness of Nick Drake or early Elliott Smith than James Taylor. And there's nothing smooth or simple about its subject matter, which revolves around the death of Stevens' mother in December 2012.

"I've grown up a lot in the past few years," says the thirty-nine-year-old singer/songwriter, sitting in his modest office overlooking the East River on a sunny, yet frigid, day earlier this month. While somber life events and the stark new album certainly back this up, his look today does not. Still boyish in a blue beanie, red sneakers, and a bright camouflage jacket, he could comfortably pass for a man ten years younger. Instruments and gear are scattered around—Stevens recorded parts of *Carrie & Lowell* by himself here during the summer as his small air conditioner whirred in the background—along with random kitsch like a copy of Christian pop icon Amy Grant's 1977 debut LP hanging on the wall, a gold-fringed hula hoop taken from a recent multimedia project he completed for the Brooklyn Academy of Music, and

a book filled with pictures of gross-out Garbage Pail Kids trading cards. A dry-erase board hosts a crude drawing of a figure with the letters "I" and "U" on either side of it and a heart in its mouth. At one point, he offers to show me his childhood stamp collection; I think he might be kidding, but he's not.

Above his computer are dozens of black binders filled with his own photos. A sampling of shots from a recent trip to Oregon shows naturescapes marked by mist and skewed tree branches and the occasional outline of a couple in the distance. "There are basically thousands and thousands of the same photograph," he says self-consciously. "They're photos your grandmother could appreciate."

There are several references to places within Oregon throughout *Carrie & Lowell*; it's where Stevens spent three summers between ages five and eight with his mother and stepfather. These early memories are not just important because they came at a formative point in Stevens' life—they're actually some of the only recollections he has of his mother, who abandoned his family when he was just a year old. Her five-year marriage to Lowell Brams in the early '80s seemingly marked a high point in a life struck by hardship; Carrie suffered from depression, schizophrenia, and alcoholism, and her contact with Stevens and his siblings, who grew up in Michigan with their dad and stepmother, was intermittent up until her death.

But there were those summers. "A lot of the best times we had while we were married were when the kids were with us," remembers the sixty-three-year-old Brams, who made a point to keep in touch with Stevens' family even after he and Carrie were divorced. He is now the director of Stevens' label, Asthmatic Kitty. "The kids were like little puppies around her, they just loved her."

Carrie & Lowell is not a sentimental affair, though. Stevens brings out all of the hurt and confusion of his relationship with his mother, as well as the debilitating aftermath of her passing, with lyrics that are poetic and unflinching. He sings of suicidal thoughts, regret, violence, brushfires, hospitals, shadows, recklessness, blood. "I just wanted to be near you," he pleads on the album, exposing the core of his own history.

"With this record, I needed to extract myself out of this environment of make-believe," he says, pulling at his sneaker's red tongue. "It's something that was necessary for me to do in the wake of my mother's death—to pursue a sense of peace and serenity in spite of suffering. It's not really trying to say anything new, or prove anything, or innovate. It feels artless, which is a good thing. This is not my art project; this is my life."

How would you describe your relationship with your mother growing up?

She left when I was one, so I have no memory of her and my father being married. She just wandered off. She felt that she wasn't equipped to raise us, so she gave us to our father. It wasn't until I was five that Carrie married Lowell. He worked in a bookstore in Eugene, Oregon, and we spent three summers out there—that's when we actually saw our mother the most.

But after she and Lowell split up, we didn't have that much contact with Carrie. Sometimes she'd be at our grandparents' house, and we'd see her during the holidays for a few days. There was the occasional letter here and there. She was off the grid for a while, she was homeless sometimes, she lived in assisted housing. There was always speculation too, like, "Where is she? What is she doing?" As a kid, of course, I had to construct some kind of narrative, so I've always had a strange relationship to the mythology of Carrie, because I have such few lived memories of my experience with her. There's such a discrepancy between my time and relationship with her, and my desire to know her and be with her.

Did you ever call her "mom" or was it always "Carrie"?

We always called our parents by their first names: Carrie and Rasjid. I'm not quite sure why.

What was Carrie like as a person?

She was evidently a great mother, according to Lowell and my father. But she suffered from schizophrenia and depression. She had bipolar disorder and she was an alcoholic. She did drugs, had substance abuse problems. She really suffered, for whatever reason. But when we were with her and when she was most stable, she was really loving and caring, and very creative and funny. This description of her reminds me of what some people have observed about my work and my manic contradiction of aesthetics: deep sorrow mixed with something provocative, playful, frantic.

Since she wasn't around that much, how did you perceive of her as a kid?

There was an awareness early on that she had schizophre-nia, suffered from depression, and that she was an alcoholic. And because both my mother and father were alcoholics and substance abuse ran in our family, when my dad got sober and started going to Alcoholics Anonymous, we all went to twelve-step meetings so we could participate in his recovery. So we had very concrete, responsible language to describe a person's struggle with addiction. We could talk about Carrie in those environments, and there was a healthy camaraderie in that culture. But I remember being a little bit embarrassed about having to go to Alateen meetings, and I didn't start drinking until I was at least of age. It was so stigmatized.

Were you there when Carrie passed away?

Yeah. She had stomach cancer, and it was a quick demise. We flew to see her in the ICU before she died. She was in a lot of pain, and on a lot of drugs, but she was aware. It was so terrifying to encounter death and have to reconcile that, and express love for someone so unfamiliar. Her death was so devastating to me because of the vacancy within me. I was trying to gather as much as I could of her, in my mind, my memory, my recollections, but I have nothing. It felt unsolvable. There is definitely a deep regret, and grief and anger. I went through all the stages of bereavement. But I say make amends while you can: take every opportunity to reconcile with those you love or those who've hurt you. It was in our best interest for our mother to abandon us. God bless her for doing that and knowing what she wasn't capable of.

That's a very Zen outlook.

Well, love is unconditional and incomprehensible. And I believe it's possible to love absent of mutual respect.

Did you feel any closure at the end—did you get to have a conversation?

For sure. At that point, I was only interested in communicating my love for her, unconditionally. There was a reciprocal deep love and care for each other in that moment. It was very profound and healing. But it's the aftermath that sucks—the emotional ramifications and repercussions that occurred for months and months following her death. It nearly destroyed me, because I still couldn't make sense out of it. In writing about it on this album, I was in pursuit of meaning, of justice, of reconciliation. It wasn't very fun.

"My imagination can be a problem. I'm prone to making my life, my family, and the world around me complicit in my cosmic fable, and often it's not fair to manipulate the hard facts of life into a vision quest." —SUFJAN STEVENS

Considering you had a distant relationship, were you at all surprised that her death hit you so hard?

Yeah. In the moment, I was stoic and phlegmatic and practical, but in the months following I was manic and frantic and disparaging and angry. They always talk about the science of bereavement, and how there is a measurable pattern and cycle of grief, but my experience was lacking in any kind of natural trajectory. It felt really sporadic and convoluted. I would have a period of rigorous, emotionless work, and then I would be struck by deep sadness triggered by something really mundane, like a dead pigeon on the subway track. Or my niece would point out polka-dotted tights at the playground, and I would suffer some kind of cosmic anguish in public. It's weird.

I was so emotionally lost and desperate for what I could no longer pursue in regard to my mother, so I was looking for that in other places. At the time, part of me felt that I was possessed by her spirit and that there were certain destructive behaviors that were manifestations of her possession.

How so?

Oh man, it's so hard to describe what was going on. It's almost like the force, or the matrix, or something: I started to believe that I was genetically, habitually, chemically predisposed to her pattern of destruction. I think a lot of the acting-out was rebellion, or maybe it was a way for me to... ah, this is so fucked up, I should probably go to therapy.

In lieu of her death, I felt a desire to be with her, so I felt like abusing drugs and alcohol and fucking around a lot and becoming reckless and hazardous was my way of being intimate with her. But I quickly learned that you don't have to be incarcerated by suffering, and that, in spite of the dysfunctional nature of your family, you are an individual in full possession of your life. I came to realize that I wasn't possessed by her, or incarcerated by her mental illness. We blame our parents for a lot of shit, for better and for worse, but it's symbiotic. Parenthood is a profound sacrifice.

The sort of rebellion you're talking about almost sounds like more of a teen-angst sort of thing.

Fun, flirty, and forty! [*laughs*] I do feel like I'm forty going on fourteen sometimes. I wasn't rebellious as a kid. I was so dignified and well-behaved. But that kind of [destructive] behavior at my age is inexcusable.

If your mother wasn't there, what was your relationship with your dad like as a kid?

Well, my siblings and I were raised like tenants, to be honest. There was a total absence of intimacy in my family, though there was still a great deal of camaraderie among the kids. Things were set up almost like a business, and it had to be managed that way because we were really poor, and there were a lot of mouths to feed. My dad and stepmom never had real, consistent careers. They were just always making ends meet. There were rules and regulations and chores, but very little time for casual enjoyment of each other's company. I don't know if that sort of ideological approach to parenting was intentional, but it's a little ironic that my closest fatherly companion is Lowell, a man who has no blood relation.

Is your dad still alive?

Yeah, but we're not that close.

Did your dad and stepmom impose Christianity onto you when you were young?

No, they weren't that religious at that time. We would go to Methodist church, because that's what my great grandmother attended. I was the acolyte in charge of lighting the candles, which was really exciting to me. I had this childhood fantasy of becoming a priest or a preacher, so I would read and study the Bible and then make my family listen to me read a passage from the New Testament before meals—and they very begrudgingly accommodated that for a while. I was just fascinated; some of my most profound spiritual and sexual experiences were at a Methodist summer camp.

As in much of your work, there are references to Christianity and mythology on this album. What does faith mean to you at this point?

I still describe myself as a Christian, and my love of God and my relationship with God is fundamental, but its manifestations in my life and the practices of it are constantly changing. I find incredible freedom in my faith. Yes, the kingdom of Christianity and the Church has been one of the most de-

structive forces in history, and there are levels of bastardization of religious beliefs. But the unique thing about Christianity is that it is so amorphous and not reductive to culture or place or anything. It's extremely malleable.

Couldn't you say that about most religions though?

Yeah, but some of them are cultural and require an allegiance to a place and a code. We live in a post-God society anyway—embrace it! [*laughs*]

A lot of people make the kind of folky music that's on this record, but so little of it actually feels meaningful; with music this spare, emotional extremity can seem like a requirement.

Yeah. Like: Don't listen to this record if you can't digest the reality of it. I'm being explicit about really horrifying experiences in my life, but my hope has always been to be responsible as an artist and to avoid indulging in my misery, or to come off as an exhibitionist. I don't want to make the listener complicit in my vulnerable prose poem of depression, I just want to honor the experience. I'm not the victim here, and I'm not seeking other peoples' sympathy. I don't blame my parents; they did the best they could.

At worst, these songs probably seem really indulgent. At their best, they should act as a testament to an experience that's universal: everyone suffers, life is pain, and death is the final punctuation at the end of that sentence, so deal with it. I really think you can manage pain and suffering by living in fullness and being true to yourself and all those seemingly vapid platitudes.

Do you think your upbringing would make you not want to have kids yourself?

Definitely. I mean, I have nieces and nephews, and there's a very clear intentionality in how they are being raised. My brother has a daughter, and she's an only child, and she's very social and outgoing and beautiful. She has lots of spirit and she knows how to use an iPad and an iPhone—she's more Internet savvy than I am and she's four years old. She's surrounded by people who love her. There's just so much intimacy. ✍

RYAN DOMBAL *is a Senior Editor at* Pitchfork.

Nothing Is Illuminated

Goodie Mob, the Atlanta Child Murders, and Hip Hop's Conspiracy of Truth

BY CHARLES AARON

ILLUSTRATIONS BY ALEXIS BEAUCLAIR

"As a rapper, how can I not believe in conspiracies? That doesn't mean I believe there's some secret room of people who had a meeting about gangsta rap, and that it was pushed... But what I do know is that I don't trust the church or the government, and anything the church or the government tells me I assume to be a lie or a conspiracy, until proven true."

—Killer Mike, *The Believer*, 2014

When someone tells me a song is "paranoid," I lean in closer. As a human being who grew up in America during the past fifty years, I *know* that certain people are after certain other people. It's written into the Constitution (or is that only in the original version that's locked in a vault under the Library of Congress?). For instance, when law enforcement officers kill African American men, and the officers' bosses then try to mislead and bully the public into believing that those men killed *themselves*, the government is essentially running a paranoia and conspiracy factory. And this ain't grandpa's seamy J. Edgar smear campaign. This is a smack in your gob. And for the families and communities of the deceased, there is no reason to believe the deaths were random acts.

When a song portrays so-called paranoia convincingly, it's an almost supernal revelation, like one of those times when feeling crazy is the least crazy emotion you can feel. That psychic come-to-Jesus shiver that atomizes the everyday nod-and-wink equilibrium. A song that infiltrates your system and unbalances your chemicals. It highlights volatile lines in your text. It scares you shitless.

Plenty of artists have wailed a "somebody's watching me" narrative, from Robert Johnson's "Hellhound on My Trail" to Black Sabbath's "Paranoid," from Michael Jackson's "Billie Jean" to Lisa Germano's *Geek the Girl* album, or Daniel Johnston's entire discography. But due to America's denial of its original and ever-evolving racist sins, African Americans have been drawn to this perspective most intensely. For an enslaved, segregated, and abused people, folklore and rumor have been essential devices for transmitting information, truths, or cries for help.

Hip hop, especially, has given paranoia and conspiracy a ferocious gutpunch. Both Lil Wayne and Kanye West (with "New Slaves" in particular) have virtually seared a defiant siege mentality into their skin; younger artists like Kevin Gates and Earl Sweatshirt seem almost preternaturally haunted. In interviews and on social media, Azealia Banks often theorizes in ways that would've been branded conspiratorial in the past, but she also provides bracing historical context where others simply troll. There's also hip-hop's ongoing evocation of the "Illuminati" (a term derived from an actual eighteenth century secret society of Bavarian elites) that's used as a catch-all for white supremacy's relentless influence and manipulation of African-American culture.

But among recent records, Kendrick Lamar's *To Pimp a Butterfly* most powerfully reflects the complex, debilitating fear that the system is not only stacked against people of color, but that an unseen hand is actively trying to contain, drive insane, or snuff out African Americans and disappear the evidence. On the album's opener, "Wesley's Theory" (inspired by the tax-related demise of Hollywood star Wesley Snipes), he raps from the point of view of America itself, a.k.a. "Uncle Sam," setting you up, stripping you down, adorning you with shiny consumer scraps, which are soon snatched back. Lamar, as Sam, taunts: "Motherfucker, you can live at the mall / Pay me later, wear those gators / But it's whatever, though, because I'm still followin' you / Hit the register, make me feel better, baby / Everything you buy, taxes will deny / I'll Wesley snipe yo ass before you're 35."

On "Hood Politics," does Kendrick propagate paranoia and conspiracy theory or just plain ass-whup logic, especially following #MichaelBrown, #TamirRice,

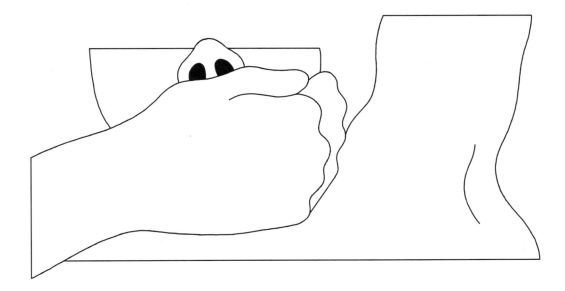

#FreddieGray, and all the dead-homie hashtags (plus the countless others not viral enough to earn anything more than a toe-tag)? Kendrick blasts: "Streets don't fail me now / They tell me it's a new gang in town / From Compton to Congress / Set-trippin' all around / Ain't nothin' but a flu of new DemoCrips and ReBloodlicans." And then the mule-kick to the head that sounds like it's straight off the protest streets of Ferguson and Baltimore: "They give us guns and drugs, call us thugs / Make it their promise to fuck with you / No condom, they fuck with you / Obama say, 'What it do?'"

Pontificators these days like to spout that there are no more musical "guilty pleasures," only "pleasures"—due to an Internet age that permits us to listen to anything at any time, thereby validating everyone's opinion. I'd suggest, at the risk of being even more glib, that for African Americans (and a great number of Americans in general), there are no more "conspiracy theories," only "theories." In an age in which we can access bulging files of information at any time from any number of sources, we question every official story, and with good reason. This is not to suggest that truth no longer exists or that African Americans no longer care about the difference between a vetted fact and a rumor, rather that conspiracy theories often contain as much (or more) truth as they do falsehood, and to focus on the flaws of the conspiracy and not the truth of the theory is bigoted in its own way.

For her 1993 book *I Heard It Through the Grapevine*, Patricia Turner, a professor at the University of California, Davis, explored the widespread African-American belief that "organized anti-black conspiracies threaten the communal well-being and, in particular, the individual bodies of blacks." Turner also pointed out this was a conviction that traced back to the country's beginnings, when "fully clothed Englishmen" and "sparsely dressed Africans" first saw each other, observed their respective "unfathomable actions," and immediately developed deep misunderstandings. Most notably, each group of strangers thought the other was going to eat them. Yes, along with slavery, fear of cannibalism was a primary orientation that whites and blacks in America shared.

This past April, University of Memphis professor Dr. Zandria Robinson, author of *This Ain't Chicago: Race, Class, and Regional Identity in the Post-Soul South*, presented a paper at the EMP Pop Conference that dug into Southern rap's preoccupation with grotesque violations of black bodies—the lynching, shackling, and bloodying by bullets, just for a start. She noted how, in "Stuntin' Like My Daddy," Lil Wayne unabashedly rapped about putting a kid's "brains on the gate" and then added, "Hey, pick 'em up / Fuck 'em, let 'em lay." She asserted that rappers make black bodies visible and visceral in order to critique the violence done against

Cee Lo Green, Khujo, T-Mo and Big Gipp of Goodie Mob, October 1995

those bodies and to express the temporal anxiety of Southern blacks who have endured the specter of historically mutilated blackness.

Dr. Robinson also talked at length about the Houston trio Geto Boys, the first and still the most compelling group to embrace and extend self-doubt, paranoia, and conspiracy to vividly passionate extremes. She ran the video for "Mind Playing Tricks on Me" and fixed on Bushwick Bill's line about pounding on the concrete during a nightmare in which he fights a towering demon until his hands bleed. Geto Boys' nightmare side is often attributed to anxiety over the so-called "gangsta lifestyle," but most pundits make this assertion blithely, not acknowledging that "gangsta" ghosts go far deeper. Robinson refers to "transhistorical violence": a horror unbound by a specific timeframe or people. Oppressed communities are always haunted by their oppressors, but the mindfuck of "Mind Playing Tricks" is that the specters haunting Geto Boys look like them; in fact, they *are* them. "Gangstas" of many eras have wrestled with this conundrum: *Am I in the life because of the system or because I'm a singular demon?*

Following the influence of Public Enemy's late-'80s world-historical consciousness and militant-pedagogical stance—which included a heavy helping of Nation of Islam conspiracy and COINTELPRO awareness—Geto Boys blew apart the lyrical possibilities of rap, commercial or otherwise. Gravediggaz' took this dark vision about as far as it could go.

Yet the most convincingly paranoid and historically wrenching version came with Goodie Mob's "Cell Therapy," from the Atlanta crew's 1995 album *Soul Food*. Rappers Khujo, Cee Lo, T-Mo, and Big Gipp bitterly spit lyrics that reference an array of systemic mindfucks: the CIA and the drug trade; child prostitution; the New World Order (see both the George H.W. Bush power grab and the theory that we're just one missile launch away from a suspension of the Constitution and installation of a one-world totalitarian government); the Klan's web of influence in local police departments as well as the FBI; discriminatory medical practices against, and the routine contamination of, African Americans (see Dr. Charles Drew being denied a blood transfusion, the Tuskegee syphilis trials, the AIDS virus); Hitler and the Nazis' concentration camps; the reinstatement of segregation/slavery via gated communities, and the prison-industrial complex (see Michelle Alexander's *The New Jim Crow*); chip implants; the income-tax bamboozle; those infernal black helicopters. A whole panoply of fuckery.

Sonically conjured by Atlanta production trio Organized Noize, "Cell Therapy" is a spare death-rattle blues, a slo-mo *vodun* funk vamp, a soggy prowl through knee-high grass. The opening's delicately staccato piano loop lures you into the darkness, crooking an index finger your way. This ain't about redemption. And the chorus introduces a trespasser whose sins definitely go unforgiven and who is given no opportunity to buy his freedom. A shotgun bursts fire into the night: "Who's that peekin' in my window / POW! / Nobody now." And with all this going on, the song still snuck onto the *Billboard* Top 40 at No. 39.

From a skeptic's distanced perspective, this might seem like just another cartoonish revenge fantasy. But for those who grew up in the primarily poor black neighborhoods in and around Atlanta during the late 1970s and early 1980s, the words rang true. For the members of Goodie Mob and Organized Noize, as well as the rest of the Dungeon Family—an extended network of Atlanta-area rappers, producers, and DJs that included OutKast (Andre 3000 makes a guest appearance elsewhere on *Soul Food*), Mr. DJ, Witchdoctor, Killer Mike, and many others—these were deathly haunting times that would be crucially formative to their conception of the world.

From the summer of 1979 to the spring of 1981, police reported as many as twenty-nine missing African American children and young adults in the Atlanta area, though later reports put the number at more than sixty possible cases. From the Eastlake Meadows projects northeast of the city to the Kimberly Courts houses in southwest Atlanta, the disappearances spanned communities from Mechanicsville to Ben Hill to East Point. Soon the dead bodies started turning up in patches of pine trees or in creeks and ditches by the side of roads. Some had been strangled. One girl was lashed to a tree. Others were found floating in the nearby South and Chattahoochee Rivers. A task force of more than one hundred law enforcement officers was formed, and a 6:00 a.m. to 6:00 p.m. curfew was instituted (which is alluded to in "Cell Therapy"). Parents were traumatized, kids contemplated the existence of a real-life boogeyman. A feeling grew that the killings were, as Nelson George wrote in his book *Post-Soul Nation: The Explosive, Contradictory, Triumphant, and Tragic 1980s*, "a kind of terror campaign against black advancement and

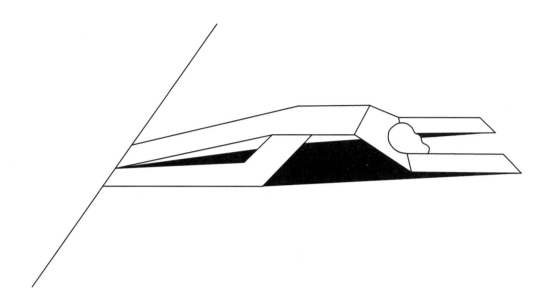

power in the heart of the South."

Organized Noize's Ray Murray put it more personally in the VH-1 documentary *ATL: The Untold Story of Atlanta's Rise in the Rap Game*: "I remember having nightmares about it as a kid, you know what I mean? Thinking somebody was gonna grab me up off the street." The reality of the times hit even closer to home for Goodie Mob's T-Mo, whose teenaged sister's body was found dumped in a creek in 1981 after being kidnapped, sexually assaulted, and shot in the head (no connection was ever found to the child-murders case). Amid all this turmoil, a mythical name developed for whoever was responsible for the kidnappings and murders: The Snatcher.

Adding suspicion to the media-fueled "black serial killer" panic, the city's administration—including its first African American mayor and an African American police chief—responded slowly to events, fretting over Atlanta's image as the gemstone of the Civil Rights movement, "the city too busy to hate," the "capital of the New South," a commercial hub booming with Coca-Cola, Delta Airlines, and several pro sports franchises. Officials dreaded the prospect of public conflict, especially after stories circulated about KKK involvement, so they downplayed the racial element. President

Jimmy Carter, a Georgia native, had to order the FBI to pursue white-supremacist leads because the local effort was lacking. As the story went national, demonstrations were held in other cities, green ribbons were worn as signs of support, and celebrities including the Jacksons, Frank Sinatra, Burt Reynolds, and Sammy Davis Jr. raised money for charities.

The murders were so symbolically disturbing that legendary African American author James Baldwin returned to the States from his self-imposed exile in Paris to report on the case. "It has something to do, in my case, with having once been a Black child in a White country," he explained. As Professor Turner writes in *I Heard It Through the Grapevine*, the fact that Atlanta was the site of these horrific murders could not be overstated. "As Baldwin notes, many black southerners proudly identify themselves with the adage, 'I'm not from Georgia, I'm from Atlanta.'" She continues:

Whereas Memphis and Dallas were perceived as racist cities when MLK and JFK were assassinated in them in the 1960s, Atlanta's reputation had improved among African-Americans. Desegregation efforts had taken well in Atlanta, a large middle-class black community thrived there[...] The home of several long-established black colleges, Atlanta was seen by many African-Americans to offer better educational and economic opportunities than any other southern or northern city.

So when an African American suspect—nerdy twenty-three-year-old fabulist Wayne B. Williams—was arrested and convicted with flimsy evidence, fear and suspicion bloomed into angry delirium. A freelance photographer and entertainment talent scout known to exaggerate his achievements, Williams was linked to no murders of children, only to the killings of two black *men* who were well into their twenties. He was also speculatively painted by the prosecution, with the help of local and national media, as a possible gay pedophile, furthering the hysteria. In short, nobody knew *what* to believe, although most saw Williams as little more than a convenient scapegoat.

Accordingly, conspiracy theories took root and spread wildly. Here's a sampling: local officials needed a black patsy to defuse possible black revolt, so they framed Williams and buried evidence against white suspects; a racist right-wing cell (KKK, Nazis, etc.) was responsible, perhaps in cahoots with police; the deaths were part of a child-pornography ring, possibly involving Williams and/or Satanists; modern-day body snatchers were killing blacks to harvest their organs; the Atlanta-based Centers for Disease Control was involved via either AIDS testing or interferon experiments, both of which were being conducted at the time. Comedian/activist Dick Gregory promoted this theory, stating that a key hormone in the latter trials was only found in, on, or near the genitalia of young black males.

The extremely public trial of Wayne Williams ended with a conviction in 1982 for the two murders that was based almost solely on circumstantial evidence. It's hard to imagine a white defendant with decent counsel being convicted and sent to prison under a similar scenario. Williams' family fought with his attorneys, the victims' families expressed doubt in Williams' guilt, and—in a move that did nothing but stoke distrust—the investigation into the other murders was closed.

A shoddy 1985 docudrama featuring Jason Robards, Morgan Freeman, James Earl Jones, Rip Torn, and Martin Sheen brought new attention to the case, which was reopened in 1987. In 1991, evidence emerged that then–assistant District Attorney William Craig had not shared with the defense team: a tape recording of known Klan member Charles T. Sanders confessing to the 1981 killing of fourteen-year-old Lubie Geter (police had used the Geter killing to establish a "pattern" that implicated Williams). The *New York Times* also reported that, according to officers of the Atlanta Bureau of Police Services and the Georgia Bureau of Investigation, the taped confession had been destroyed and other portions of the investigative file had been lost.

Clearly, conspiracy theories are stories we develop and tell each to explain the unexplained or unspeakable; they're a way we try and mediate our pain and despair about injustice and lost innocence. But that doesn't mean they should be dismissed. It's certainly no surprise that by 1995, Goodie Mob and the Dungeon Family—having survived the child-murders monstrousness, the crack-era blight, Reagan sentencing hysteria and Clinton "welfare reform," not to mention the usual racism and imperialism—would be doubtful of official accounts and put forward a defensive-yet-aggressive, provocatively ominous point of view. On *Soul Food*'s "Thought Process," Andre 3000 laments: "Nobody would die in cops and robbers when we used to play, right? / Huh, the only thing we feared was Williams, Wayne / Never thought about hittin' licks and slangin' cane."

James Baldwin, in his book-length essay about the Atlanta child murders, *The Evidence of Things Not Seen*, writes:

Terror cannot be remembered. One blots it out. The organism—the human being—blots it out. One invents, or creates, a personality or persona. Beneath this accumulation (rock of Ages!) sleeps or hopes to sleep, that terror which the memory repudiates. Yet, it never sleeps—that terror, which is not the terror of death (which cannot be imagined) but the terror of being destroyed.

That terror is still with us. Some of hip-hop's most prominent artists are still defined, in large part, by their immersion in very real paranoia and conspiracy, which says a lot about our country's brutally contested history. Despite the rapid evolution of information and its supposed availability, this also speaks to how little any of us truly know. As the songs tell us, we're making mystery as much as history. ✐

CHARLES AARON *is former Editorial Director of* SPIN *magazine. He now lives and writes in Durham, N.C.*

Visions of War

Punk's Obsession with the Aesthetics of Conflict

BY DAN TROMBLY

Joe Strummer, 1984, Spain. Photograph by Juan Jesús García

Violence, in the classic trope of military history, is a tool for sorting out victors from vanquished, living from dead, and disputed questions from settled ones. In the case of hardcore scenes in the early 1980s, it was a tool for sorting out poseurs from punks. "We were trying to stand out, and the one way it seemed [that worked] at the time was violence... The violence was one way to ratchet it up, to make it too unpleasant to people who weren't really down," recounted D.C. punk icon Ian MacKaye to Michael Azerrad in *Our Band Could Be Your Life*. MacKaye was anti–war and, by the time the D.C. hardcore community realized it could no longer control the violent tendencies it had unleashed, he had also become steadfastly opposed to the belligerent practices that came to dominate shows. But it's no surprise that violence, as a stylistic signal used in the local brawling of punk concerts or invoked through global wars in punk lyrics, is so popular: it pervades cultures and polarizes them, it shocks and unfailingly triggers emotional response.

Although MacKaye renounced violence as an instrument of scene policy, its early prominence recalls a founding myth of so many artistic movements of the young and disillusioned: the need to break with convention so sharply as to stand apart even from those people, whether they're from the mainstream or are fellow dissidents, who are too soft or too prone to selling out. In one generation, a subculture declared: "We intend to exalt aggressive action, a feverish insomnia... the punch and the slap." Tired of living by the accepted conventions of their craft and their society, they asked, "But who cares? We don't want to understand!" The Italian Futurists' joyous and dangerous irreverence was the product of post-World War I Italy rather than Cold War Britain and America, but that sentiment echoed. Modern events render societal norms absurd, and those who coped by smiling had to make way for those who were swinging.

These moments of purposeful nihilism and combative stylings were backed by a full-throated ideology of war and a reactionary contempt for other social movements, but they shared their fascination with speed, novelty, and violent power with many beyond their subcultural clique. As poetry scholar Marjorie Bertloff noted of the avant-garde artists who experienced or reckoned with the Great War, conflict, with all its transformational power and shocking acceleration of modern forces, captivated artists dissatisfied with the conventions of pre-war Europe. Italian Futurists, for example, extolled the virtues of "energy, violent transformation, vision, techno-culture, [and] rejection of the past," and these war- and modernity-awed sentiments had their echoes in punk rock decades later. Just as the concept of the vanguard's subversive potential informed the language and images of underground and rebellion in punk rock, the artistic avant-garde demonstrated how war, as a chaotic force, held innate appeal to alienated kids, nihilistic and bored in the face of tradition—in other words, the counterculture punk emerged from.

The self-image of many punk and post-punk bands originates in ideas conceptually and historically indebted to the influence of violence and war, including the idea of "underground" activity, rebellion, and subversion. In practice, punk and post-punk developed in a historical context between two world wars—a remembered Second and an expected Third—where underground action, rebellion, and subversion were ubiquitous elements of modern life.

The eminent historian Tony Judt, in *Postwar*, his history of Europe after 1945, dismissed punk rock by way of the Sex Pistols: their "politics were as one-dimensional as their musical range, the latter all too often restricted to three chords and a single beat and dependent upon volume for its effect. Like the Red Army Faction, the Sex Pistols and other punk rock groups wanted above all to shock." To Judt, punk was an "evisceration of musical form," as "bogus" as its ideology. Although the early wave of British punk fell short of the intellectual historian's standards, his comparison to Germany's Red Army Faction would ring true for many punk bands of the '70s and early '80s.

The Red Army Faction (also known as the RAF, or by the state and media's more pejorative Baader-Meinhof Gang after two of its founders, Andreas Baader and Ulrike Meinhof) emerged from a disillusionment with modernity as young Germans coming of age after World War II reckoned with an unsatisfying present and an inescapable past. Their parents' generation produced fascism, their government and elites were either participants or complicit in Nazi rule, and the idealistic student movements of the 1960s and 1970s had left the radical left impotent. Violence—the "propaganda of the deed"—soon became an increasingly chic persuasion among the young. The first RAF wave robbed banks to fund bombings, a campaign that captured public attention but landed most of them in prison by the early 1970s.

By the time "Anarchy in the UK" came out in 1977, the original generation of RAF members were already imprisoned. Within a year, new followers had taken up the cause and done so with vigor: shooting a banker in a failed kidnapping, then abducting an ex-Nazi industrialist, shooting his bodyguard and police in the process. The kidnappers demanded the release of RAF prisoners in exchange for the industrialist. Sympathizers and collaborators in the anti-capitalist, anti-imperialist struggle, Palestinian Liberation Organization members hijacked a Lufthansa flight and amplified those demands. They executed its captain before German authorities ultimately stormed the aircraft. Soon after news reached Germany, imprisoned RAF members supposedly participated in a coordinated suicide attempt, although one survivor claims it was government assassination. The RAF executed their industrialist hostage soon afterwards.

Amid the bloodshed in 1978, the Clash's Joe Strummer (who frequently performed in a T-shirt featuring logos of the RAF and kindred Italian revolutionaries Brigate Rosse) declared to *Melody Maker*, "You've got to hand it to [the RAF], putting their lives on the line for the human race." Although his bandmates did not necessarily share Strummer's politics—and Strummer himself ostensibly qualified his enthusiasm for militancy with his critique of revolutionary vanity in "Tommy Gun" —the symbolic allure remained: *Sandinista!* (1980) took its title and catalogue number (FSLN1) from Nicaragua's revolutionaries-turned-rulers, the Frente Sandinista de Liberación Nacional, while *Combat Rock* (1982) took its catalogue number (FMLN2) from El Salvador's guerrilla coalition, Frente Farabundo Martí para la Liberación Nacional. While resistance to the military government and coup-plagued regime of El Salvador or to the dictatorship of Nicaragua's Somoza family was undoubtedly a less ambiguous cause than the hostage-taking and assassinations in democratic West Germany, the Clash's serial incorporation of guerrilla chic provided an archetype for the way thumbing noses at American-backed counterinsurgency campaigns also makes for good countercultural branding.

WWII dealt a crippling blow to European colonial powers and set the stage for an era of worldwide revolutionary activity, and it's easy to see why the groups that emerged during this time were both ideologically and conceptually attractive to punks. The archetypal clandestine militant organization is a community united against the common foe of an oppressive system; it bears the frustration of impotent dissent alongside a desire to shatter the complacent illusions of the masses and build something new upon the ruins of the old. However, while bands such as the Clash explicitly incorporated tropes of violent rebellion into their artistic rebellion, for the majority of British and American punk bands (save perhaps Northern Irish acts like Stiff Little Fingers, the Undertones, or Ruefrex), war remained an exoticism or an interrupting shock rather than a daily concern.

That same contrast to normal life's doldrums also drove media fixation on conflict. Beyond the obvious political stakes of covering the global Cold War, war holds for many audiences a spectacular appeal. Even some of the most damning antiwar accounts still hold immense aesthetic power. As a showcase of the extreme, the inhuman scale of violence and the intensely human experiences of dealing with and facing it, war has been a subject of enduring appeal for many artists beyond various wars'

particular politics. In an era of televised bloodshed, punk brought in an awareness of both the horror and the way this spectacle was a cultural product.

Leeds' Gang of Four took their name from the Maoist architects of China's totalitarian purges, and their songs delivered a chilling assessment of the Western world's gaze on the Cold War's hot fringes of proxy warfare. 1979's *Entertainment!* aimed Marxist-inflected barbs at a variety of targets, from Britain's post-imperial identity crises to the dancefloor anxieties of commodified sexuality. Gang of Four went beyond the basic condemnation of capitalism and imperialism as exploitative systems and examined how they perpetuated themselves through cultural representation and consumption. Their song "5.45," unmistakably indebted to news coverage of civil war and violent repression in Central American and other third-world nations, shows these conflicts not just as struggles between combatants but as a mediated relationship between Western viewers and the violence itself.

The months before *Entertainment!*'s release were turbulent ones in Nicaragua, where it became increasingly clear that, despite the United States' terminating aid to the Somoza regime two years prior, the government and the country's US-trained National Guard would not permit the Somoza regime to end peacefully. The repressive brutality became painfully clear to Western eyes in June 1979, when National Guard troops pulled ABC journalist Bill Stewart and his interpreter Juan Francisco Espinosa out of their van at a checkpoint and executed them. Stewart's death, surreptitiously captured on camera, showed him obediently prostrating himself as a soldier casually walked over and shot him in the head. The footage aired on all major American networks as well as many others worldwide, and it stands as the kind of jarring moment in televised violence that "5.45" presents as increasingly routine. "How can I sit and eat my tea / With all that blood flowing from the television?" asks guitarist Andy Gill in a resigned monotone. The band numbly continues, "Watch new blood on the 18-inch screen / The corpse is a new personality / Ionic charge gives immortality / The corpse is a new personality." The song ends with a repeated declaration that sounds, like so many other Gang of Four lyrics, like a revolutionary cadre's attempt at an advertising jingle: "Guerrilla war struggle is a new entertainment."

As the National Guard's brutal executions demonstrated their view of the global media as an adversary

VIOLENCE—
THE "PROPAGANDA
OF THE DEED"—
SOON BECAME AN
INCREASINGLY CHIC
PERSUASION AMONG
THE YOUNG.

ALIENATED KIDS,
NIHILISTIC & BORED
IN THE FACE OF
TRADITION

in the contest for public opinion, Gang of Four's song demonstrates how media production and consumption discolor and repackage political violence for faraway viewers in ways that capture viewers' attention without requiring much context. More than a decade before *Entertainment!*, the Vietnam War provided a similarly striking image when photographer Eddie Adams captured the execution of Viet Cong (or National Liberation Front, as they more often called themselves) operative Nguyen Van Lém by South Vietnamese National Police Chief Nguyen Ngoc Loan. Viewers do not need to know the context for the image to have a visceral impact; they do not need to know about the February 1968 Tet Offensive that brought bloody street fighting to bustling Saigon, or about Loan's dead men and the guerrilla execution of South Vietnamese civilian collaborators in Saigon or Hue, or much about Lém or his movement at all.

In 1973, as America's frontline involvement in Vietnam drew to a long-awaited close, the Stooges released *Raw Power*. Both band and album are well-known symbols of the kind of nihilism and violent energy punk became famous for, but one song stands out as a particularly effective example of how the genre galvanized warfare into its treatment of these themes. "Search and Destroy" took its name from a concept popularized in United States doctrine during Vietnam, where airmobile units went looking for the enemy (or, put more simply, looking for action); the phrase served as a stand-in for the manner of prowling for debauchery and violence cultivated by punk in general and Iggy in particular. In the song, Iggy howls a cartoonish parody of military terminology as he walks the street with "a heart full of napalm," seeking "love in the middle of a firefight." When he warns, "Look out honey, 'cause I'm using technology," he evokes a common theme in early punk and avant-garde modernism: the idea of pushing modern technology past its intended limits and uses.

This theme would be taken up by fellow Midwestern punks David Thomas and Peter Laughner in their post–Rocket from the Tombs outfit, Pere Ubu, a band steeped in avant-garde aesthetics and, in some early works, the imagery of modern war. Pere Ubu's debut single, "30 Seconds Over Tokyo," depicts Lieutenant Colonel Jimmy Doolittle's audacious 1942 one-way bombing raid against the Japanese capital. Through a six-minute epic that mixes psychedelic riffing and passages of atonal cacophony, listeners navigate a wartime soundscape guided by Thomas' tale of "dark flak spiders" and "toy city streets crawling through my sights." Doolittle's raid pushed the mechanical capability of his aircraft in order to symbolically bring war to the heart of Japan; Pere Ubu's bold act of noise engineering gives the operation an almost transcendent quality.

Pere Ubu's invocation of wartime imagery continued in 1978's "Non-Alignment Pact." Fashioning international diplomacy into a metaphor for romantic turmoil, Thomas warns, "At night I can see the stars on fire / I can see the world in flames / And it's all because of you / Or your thousand other names." Pere Ubu's use of international calamities to illustrate inner life rather than ideological claims is an early example of what would become a prominent feature in post-punk lyrics. But Pere Ubu, like many thematic imitators, were also early cases of how bands could land in hot water for invoking memories of atrocity. In "Final Solution," Thomas bemoans the usual punk themes, saying, "Mamma threw me out till I get some pants that fit / She just won't approve of my strange kind of wit." But from there he leaps into darker language, claiming that he doesn't need a cure but "a final solution," and finds solace in the shows where "guitar's gonna sound like a nuclear destruction," with a rumbling blast filling a pause for emphasis. Thomas claims that "Final Solution" is a reference to the Sherlock Holmes mystery "The Final Problem" rather than the Holocaust (though it's difficult to imagine that a band familiar with the intricacies of the Doolittle Raid was unaware of the resonance of WWII's gravest crime), but nevertheless he suspended live performances of the song out of sensitivity to the inescapable connotations of the phrase.

With Joy Division, whose morose post-punk owes some inspiration to Pere Ubu, there is no disputing the use of Nazi terms and imagery. The band's name comes from the infamous book *The House of Dolls*, an account of forced Jewish prostitution in Auschwitz that contains lurid depictions of violence and sexuality that critics found exploitative and scholars now regard as fictionalized. The artwork for their 1978 EP, *An Ideal for Living*, features a Hitler Youth drummer boy and elements of an infamous photo of the SS corralling Jewish women and children at gunpoint during the 1943 Warsaw Ghetto Uprising. Their song "Warsaw" is an explicit account of Adolf Hitler's Deputy Führer Rudolf Hess, who fell out of favor and attempted to negotiate a separate peace with the British after Germany's 1941 opening of a second front against the Soviet Union, only to be imprisoned in Scotland. A second song on that EP, "No

Love Lost," explicitly deals with *The House of Dolls*' subject matter and even includes a direct quotation. Joy Division would back off from nakedly fascistic album packaging, but they remained engrossed with fascism. Another song, "They Walked In Line," specifically depicts the mentality of war criminals "all dressed in uniforms so fine," demonstrating both a morbid interest in modern inhumanity and the aesthetics of the perpetrators.

Joy Division's reasons for prominently showcasing uniformed murderers have been varied: Guitarist Bernard Sumner and bassist Peter Hook both admitted their curiosity about fascist aesthetics; vocalist Ian Curtis' struggles with epilepsy, infidelity, and depression suggested a draw toward a subject matter that would allow him to explore deep feelings of alienation, turmoil, and melancholy. As Michael Bibby suggested in his essay on Joy Division's influence in gothic subcultures, the line "For entertainment they watch his body twist," from the song "Atrocity Exhibition," could refer equally well to oppression's audience and to Curtis' own audience, watching his seizures onstage and mistaking "the real and painful experience of his condition" for merely a stylized act.

Joy Division's references to Nazism were all the more disturbing given the shift in the UK's contemporary fascist culture from provocation to violent practice. In the 1970s, sporting swastikas was a routine punk shock tactic: a cursory image search shows members of the Stooges, the Sex Pistols, Siouxsie and the Banshees, and the Exploited wearing swastikas or other Nazi paraphernalia. The intent was to shock the bourgeois through ugly, ignorant symbolism, however, by the late 1970s and early 1980s, it was increasingly difficult to argue that invoking a resurgent far-right movement was particularly subversive. The 1970s saw a disturbing rise in white nationalism in Britain, with parties such as the National Front promoting xenophobia toward non-white citizens. As competing rallies between the National Front and anti-fascist groups began to result in street violence, the clash between the far right and its opponents became not just historical curiosity but reality.

Ian Curtis' suicide in 1980 prompted the band to rename itself New Order, a name that referred not to Nazi geopolitical fantasy, but rather to an article about the People's New Order of Kampuchea—as if invoking Pol Pot or the recent violent overthrow of his genocidal regime would be less disturbing. Regardless of the origin of its name, New Order demonstrated a growing trend in which

post-punk put "Atrocity Exhibition" into artistic practice. Beyond the historical specifics of the two totalitarian regimes, Joy Division, New Order, and many other post-punk bands flirted with totalitarian symbols and ideas, capitalizing on the aesthetic draw of violent movements and their actions.

Corpses and other images of violence are integral to most reckonings with war, but depicting these sorts of graphic horrors can be as essentializing as it is essential, regardless of political intent. Discharge—a UK punk band so critical to the anti-war, d-beat punk aesthetic that its sleeve style, font, and Dis- prefix haunts the 7-inch crates of any punk savvy record store—provides a classic example of how graphic imagery meant to appall and mobilize can become an aesthetic convention. Their 1981 album *Why* relentlessly catalogued brutalities and pacifistic desperation. The album art features, among other images of violence, corpses strewn on the ground during the Japanese Army's genocidal 1937 sacking of Nanking, China, and a photo taken of bombs falling from a WWII air raid. Their 1984 compilation *Never Again* invoked the titular anti-genocide slogan and cribbed the image of a dove of peace impaled on a bayonet from artist John Heartfield's montage *The Meaning of Geneva, Where Capital Lives, Cannot Live Peace!*

Discharge's pastiche of wars past, present, and future is reinforced by their minimalist approach to lyrics. Each song is a sparse, brutal depiction of repression or atrocity. "Mania For Conquest" provides a strong example:

In order to satisfy their mania for conquest
Lives are squandered
To satisfy their mania, mania for conquest

Civilians torn from their families
Happy homes destroyed
And for what
To satisfy their mania, mania for conquest

Discharge's critique goes beyond any particular policy or historical moment, and their anarchism indicted war and government wholesale. "Mania For Conquest" could describe any war. "Kept in line with truncheons, rifle butts and truncheons," from "State Violence, State Control," could describe virtually any state. In their artwork and lyrics, Discharge, as well as the d-beat and raw

FOR D-BEAT AND
OTHER ANARCHO
PUNKS, THE IMAGERY
OF WAR'S ABYSS
BECOMES A USEFUL
SIGNAL OF KINSHIP,
A CURRENCY OF AES-
THETIC CREDIBILITY
WHOSE DARK ALLURE
IS IMMEDIATE AND
VISCERAL.

punks that emulated their template, turn the memories and photographic artifacts of specific historical contexts into a collage that collapses all warfare and government into an indistinguishable series of crimes that inevitably culminates in a mushroom cloud.

When Discharge wrote "Realities of War," they meant to dispel romantic illusions, but (as previous generations of artists discovered) highlighting war's realities permits aesthetic ambiguity. In Sweden, where Discharge spawned myriad imitators, the term *kängpunk*—or "boot punk," after the steel-toed and military-style footwear preference of musicians and fans—came to define a broadly anarcho-pacifist genre. Go to a d-beat hardcore show today and you're sure to find some punks festooned in military-style boots, modified fatigues, or perhaps even belts made of gleaming faux machine-gun ammunition. Similarly, you needn't look too far to find 7" sleeves depicting monochrome photocopies of smoldering cities, gas-masked rituals of apocalyptic preparation, and dead bodies. For d-beat and other anarcho punks, the imagery of war's abyss becomes a useful signal of kinship, a currency of aesthetic credibility whose dark allure is immediate and visceral.

Where d-beat appropriated wartime imagery as a radical critique of government and violence, Oi! music and far-right politics acquired a discomfortingly intermingled reputation. Oi! bands (much like the British working class itself) ran the political gamut but generally shared an interest in sport, enthusiasm for street-fighting, anger with the political establishment, and a disdain for law enforcement. Songs like Cock Sparrer's "England Belongs to Me" and the Angelic Upstarts' "England" were populist anthems patriotic enough to attract the interest of the far right despite the band's own political affiliations or the lyrical intent of the songs themselves (to wit: Cock Sparrer counted a self-described Trotskyite socialist as a former manager, and the Upstarts' anthem commemorates those who died fighting Nazis).

Political ambiguity on the parts of listeners and bands was endemic to Oi! and punk music at that time. Combat 84, an undeniably right-wing band, would demand "bigger and better bombs" in their song "Right to Choose," while lamenting British troops dying in pointless conflicts in the song "Soldier." For the most part, the violence that Combat 84 fans faced in their daily lives stemmed from an overlap of hooligan violence and politicized streetfighting—as

the Ejected would describe it in "Gang Warfare"—that turned "boredom" into "world war," with participants dressing to match. Combat 84 described the skinhead aesthetic in a self-titled song, raging: "Ten-hole DMs on your feet / Well polished and looking neat / Paramilitary is the score / We're the band Combat 84."

In the song "Violence," they go even further: "People never learn however much you try / There's violence in your blood so someone's gotta die." It's debatable whether the aesthetics of the subculture led Oi! bands to right-wing politics and an endorsement of street violence, or vice versa. Either way, Oi! music provides a clear example of the way in which punk links subcultural style with political violence. "Apolitical" bands were steeped in political messaging and posturing whether they admitted it or not, and the ideology of the self-avowedly political was not always as steadfast as it might seem.

In their 1978 *No Town Hall* 7-inch, post-punk band Crisis decry the neo-Nazism and Holocaust denialism hiding in British nationalism's increasingly mainstream rhetoric: "You read in it in a book / Seen it on the TV screen / To you it's a nightmare / But to some it's a dream." Similarly, "Red Brigades," their critique of Italian militants, was centered on urban terrorism's likelihood to empower neo-fascists rather than an outright condemnation of the type of violence in which Crisis fans reputedly partook during confrontations with far-right skinheads at shows. With their subsequent band, Death In June, ex-Crisis members Douglas Pearce and Tony Wakeford became case studies in how post-punk musicians became absorbed in the fascist images and themes.

Ostensibly a post-punk/neofolk project, Death in June's aesthetic is replete with fascist symbols, Nazi military uniforms, and pseudo-occult or paganistic imagery intended to accentuate an imagined European heritage. Pearce, when asked in interviews about the transition toward explicitly fascist imagery, has argued that by the time of their last shows in 1980, Crisis was already making "Music to March To" and wearing fatigues onstage—though he has also attributed the shift in his political views to the discovery of more left-leaning factions of the Nazi Party that were purged on June 30, 1934. Drawing the line between aesthetic interest and political allure is a difficult task for many Death in June fans, and the band's influence can be felt throughout modern day industrial, punk, and post-punk. Their esoteric fascist alternative may hold some appeal to those who consider themselves too sophisticated for the more stereotypical bloody-knuckled white power lifestyle, but for many fans a t-shirt with Death in June's SS logo provides the same subversive thrill experienced by fans of numerous other bands whose iconography is steeped in ambiguous images of atrocity.

Death In June's totalitarian sensationalism has become ingrained in current neo-folk and industrial music by subduing its most provocative qualities while its fascist imagery is justified as genre convention, tribute, or artistic subversion. The Brooklyn record store Heaven Street, run by Sean Ragon of Cult of Youth, takes its name from a Death in June song about the Nazis' Sobibór death camp. Similarly, Denmark's Iceage—who were teenagers when 2011's *New Brigade* skyrocketed them to international fame—demonstrates how fascist imagery has become a routine and recurring presence in punk aesthetics.

Although the band has vocally distanced themselves from fascism in interviews, *New Brigade*'s Klan-like imagery revealed their post-punk fixation with fascism and a tendency toward juvenile provocation. Similarly, the song "Everything Drifts," off their second LP, *You're Nothing*, reminds us why and how a fascination with violence and totalitarianism became so embedded in the genre in the first place. Frontman Elias Rønnenfelt asks in the first verse, "Maybe we were made for this / Causing harm," building to the more emphatic demand:

Everything drifts
Soon it's gone
Don't find a place to stay
Nature is violence
Bow in its grace

It's a more elegant reinterpretation of Combat 84's "Violence," echoing eighteenth-century reactionary thinker Joseph de Maistre when he wrote, "All creation groans… toward another order of things." While Maistre's elegy to violence was part of a coherent doctrine of political thought, war-fixated artists from the avant-garde and punk nihilists have demonstrated that the undeniable excitement of violent aesthetics need not be tied to a specific ideology, and have subsequently broadened the appeal of such acts over and over again.

While specific wars and the concept of war in general

may provide ripe subject matter or stylistic inspiration, it is difficult for bands to draw from these depths without treading on the historical memories of others. Take, for example, many North American artists, especially those young enough to only know the Vietnam War from movies or from deciphering its slang from bands like Fugazi (whose name is the acronym for "Fucked Up, Got Ambushed, Zipped In[to a bodybag]'). The death toll of the decades-long conflict that saw communist forces unite Vietnam at gunpoint includes millions of Vietnamese, Laotians, and Cambodians, along with thousands of extra-regional combatants, including Americans, Australians, and South Koreans. Like most civil wars, the human cost of the war in Indochina fell mostly on local civilians. Calgary post-punk band Viet Cong—after facing media criticism and a highly publicized show cancellation—insist that none of this was on their mind when they chose that name. It has been explained at various times as a cringe-inducing reference to the bassist's playing style—one befitting a Kalashnikov-wielding, "rice paddy hat"–wearing insurgent—their love of Vietnam War movies, or a fitting description of their "explosive and dark" sound. However, as Sang Nguyen described in a letter to the band published on the *Impose Magazine* website, she (like so many others who fled as the war's final phase of violent purging and power consolidation cemented the communists' control of southern Vietnam) cannot separate the band's name from the reality of her experiences.

So long as punk bands keep reacting to politics and politics keep involving violence, there will be plenty of music delving into imagery of mass graves and rebel fighters. To evaluate these bands and know where they stand is a relatively straightforward matter. But for a genre prone to recycling the experiences and suffering of others into a good metaphor or compelling image, it is important to recognize that "apolitical" uses of political violence require ignoring the historic context both of the actions referenced and of punk and art's relationship with war in general. Almost a half century after the ascent of punk in pop culture, the subversive pose has now become a traditionalist's defensive crouch. "5.45" was released in 1979, and "guerrilla war struggle" is now an old entertainment indeed. ✎

DAN TROMBLY *is a DC-based writer and researcher focusing on conflict and security.*

As Much As I Can, As Black As I Am

The Queer History of Grace Jones

BY BARRY WALTERS

ILLUSTRATIONS BY HATTIE STEWART

Grace Jones is perched on a ledge above the dance-floor of New York's 12 West, the state-of-the-art, members-only gay disco, about to take the stage for one of her first performances. The year is 1977, and the club's venerated DJ Jimmy Stuard has been pumping an instrumental version of a track that was about to be released under Jones' name. No one was prepared for what was about to hit them.

Tom Moulton, father of the dance mix, whose first disco productions were Jones' earliest hits, describes the scene at 12 West: "All of a sudden the spotlight hits her. She starts singing 'I Need a Man,' and the place goes crazy. After she finishes, she goes, 'I don't know about you, honey, but *I need a fucking man!*' You talk about a room-worker. *Whatever it takes.* She was so determined."

To understand the seismic impact of this moment, one must understand a bit of history. Just a few years earlier, it had been illegal in NYC for two men to so much as dance together. With the exception of maybe hairdressers and artists, queer people risked unemployment if they so much as hinted at their orientation outside the confines of gay bars and clubs, and it was in these discos that the seeds of liberation were sown. At 12 West, gay people could grasp the power of their collectivity and understand what it meant to be free.

Tough and lusty, Grace Jones sang "I Need a Man" just like a man might, a woman who was not just singing *to* them, but also *for* them, *as* them. Jones, an icon and cultural force, is as queer as a relatively straight person gets. Her image, at once, celebrated blackness and subverted gender norms; she presented something we had never seen before in pop performance--a woman who was lithe, sexy, hyperfeminine and exuded a ribald, butch swagger. She holds herself like royalty and flaunts transgressive charisma so blindingly bold that, even in 2015, she's still *outré*. Back in '79, *Ebony* got Jones' *je ne sais quoi* exactly right: "Grace Jones is a question mark followed by an exclamation point."

In 1960, a twelve-year-old Beverly Grace Jones moved from Spanish Town, Jamaica, where they'd grown, up to Syracuse, New York, with her family. She didn't have many friends; a high school report card described her as "socially sick." Halfway through Syracuse University, she impulsively abandoned her studies to work on a play in Philadelphia. The Pentecostal preacher's daughter realized there was no going home after that; she moved to New York City in 1975 to fulfill her dream of becoming a star.

At first, Jones modeled for the Wilhelmina Agency while doubling as a go-go dancer under the pseudonym Grace Mendoza. "Even though the agency kept me pretty busy, I auditioned for every play and film I could find," the *Baltimore Afro American* quoted her in 1985. "But they all wanted a black American sound, and I just didn't have it. Finally, I got tired of trotting around, and took myself to Paris."

There her blackness set her apart from other models, and Jones landed covers of *Stern*, *Pravda*, and *Vogue*. Within a few months she recorded a few singles; one was sent to Cy and Eileen Berlin, an enterprising husband-and-wife team who later managed Tom Cruise. Jones flew back to NYC with her roommate, actress Jessica Lange, and met with the Berlins. Impressed by her exuberance, star quality, and willingness, they signed on to manage her. "I thought of her as family," says Eileen Berlin. "She had given up their apartment; my son had gone to college, and so I gave her his room."

The year before, Tom Moulton had created the first nonstop disco LP side for Gloria Gaynor's smash "Never Can Say Goodbye," and pioneered the earliest club-specific mixes that were then blowing up both discos and R&B radio. The Berlins begged Moulton to produce their new client, Grace Jones. He initially demurred: he preferred to tinker with finished tapes to heighten their danceability and radiance rather than create the initial work.

Despite his reservations, he took Jones on. Their partnership initially began with "Sorry" / "That's the Trouble," a double-sided '76 disco hit Jones had co-written and originally recorded in Paris, that was issued stateside on the Berlins' Beam Junction label with artwork by *Interview*'s Richard Bernstein. Their next collaboration, "I

Need a Man," quickly rose to the top of Billboard's disco chart in '77. The Berlins hoped to capitalize on Jones' burgeoning fame and approached Island Records founder Chris Blackwell about signing her, which he did in short order. Given Blackwell's status as an international reggae ambassador and the singer's Jamaican roots, Cy Berlin anticipated a good fit. He didn't know how right he'd be.

Although Moulton and Jones made three albums together in three years—'77's *Portfolio*, '78's *Fame*, and '79's *Muse*—the two former-models often clashed. "I always teased her about sounding like Bela Lugosi," recalls the disco godfather. "I stood next to her while she was singing because I got so sick of hitting the talkback button [in the control room]. The moment she'd go off, I'd stop her. I was hard on her, I really was, but she had that determination. No matter how much I pushed her, she would take it and push herself." Jones took vocal lessons twice a week.

Fashioned after his Gaynor medleys, *Portfolio*'s continuous first side features Broadway tunes set to string-intensive bluster arranged by the Salsoul Orchestra's Vince Montana and performed by members of MFSB, an uncommonly cohesive pool of studio musicians who played on nearly every Philadelphia-originated soul hit of the '70s. Against the plush effortlessness, Jones sounds strained; the weight of Moulton's hand is audible, how hard he was pushing her is uncomfortable to hear. However, the LP's single-packed second side dished out a masterstroke in Jones' take on Édith Piaf's "La Vie En Rose," a version of which Moulton had previously recorded with forgotten '70s singer Teresa Wiater.

Jones had gotten her hands on an acetate pressing of Waiter's unreleased recording, which had been wowing the 12 West crowd, and she lobbied Moulton to let her have it, baiting him that it would be a sure hit for the two: "I'm big in France." The same rawness and struggle that works against Jones on Broadway arias here conveys the absolute heartbreak of the Piaf original.

On Jones' second album, *Fame*, Moulton bolstered the French connection: most songs were written by Jack Robinson and Jacques Pépino (credited as James Bolden, but elsewhere known as disco singer David Christie). Once again Moulton contrasts Philly soul's lush romanticism—here even more effusive, thanks to arranger John Davis, also a hot producer and bandleader—with Jones'

ERIC SHOREY ON "WARM LEATHERETTE"

Grace Jones' cover of The Normal's "Warm Leatherette", is one of her more bizarre interpretations. The original song, based on the dystopian novel *Crash* by J.G. Ballard, was a cold proto-industrial track riffing on the flattening of human affect due to post-modern technology. The original book—about a man who awakens from a near fatal car crash to find himself only sexually aroused by automotive manslaughter—inspired countless queer Electroclash superstars, but Jones' version remains the most unique.

In Jones' hands, the song becomes a sassy tribute to the pleasures of ultraviolence, queering the original text from a self-serious and mega-ironic love poem into a campy exploration of black female sexual identity. By subverting the tropes of white, male, anglo sci-fi, Jones turned the Ballardian porno-nightmare into a celebration of perversion via the intersection of technology and sexuality.

JES SKOLNIK ON "USE ME"

Grace Jones' version of Bill Withers' "Use Me" is exactly what a cover song should be: it honors the strengths of the original while restructuring it, truly taking possession of it as if it were her own work. While Withers' original is full of human pain and love, Jones' version–produced by Sly and Robbie for Nightclubbing–turns on one robotic heel into S&M, all sex, all strength. The distinctly American, organic funk of the original is refashioned as electro-Caribbean minimalism, letting Jones' voice be as powerful as Withers'. In both versions, it is the voice that holds this song together. When issued from Jones' lips, "use me up" becomes a challenge: a love song for power bottoms everywhere.

confident, almost stentorian vocals. This time around, though, that combination gels throughout because the material is made for her. Jones dedicates the album "with love" to her then-partner, Jean-Paul Goude, a Parisian multimedia artist who collaborated with her on the creation of subsequent album jackets, photos, videos, and stage shows. (Goude is also the father of her only child and author of a book that details their relationship, *Jungle Fever*.)

While the follow up, *Muse*, didn't yield as many memorable songs, it did feature another nonstop A side, one that moves from sin to salvation via stormy arrangements by Iceland's Thor Baldursson, whose keyboards and charts lit up Giorgio Moroder and Boney M songs alike. It also brandished a killer floor-filler, "On Your Knees." Laced with sadistic intent by D.C. LaRue (a cult disco act whose world-weary, gay-coded "Cathedrals" presaged Pet Shop Boys) and former Sugarloaf frontman Jerry Corbetta, the most soulful of Jones' disco singles also points toward her future. The philharmonic instrumentation still oozes luxury, but the swagger of the lyric and the toughness of her vocal suggests rock 'n' roll dissent waiting to be unleashed.

I grew up in Rochester, New York, ninety miles from where a teenaged Grace Jones was realizing her grand ambitions. I was a fan of the city's punk band, New Math, whose Kevin Patrick did promo for Island and passed me a copy of *Fame* (it was the first piece of my disco vinyl collection, which now numbers in the thousands.) Later that week, I watched Jones on *The Midnight Special*, where she performed "Below The Belt," the only *Fame* track that Jones is credited with co-writing. She took the stage clad in a pearly satin boxing robe and a training belt, her hands taped for a fight. Halfway through, she pulled a brawny muscleman onto the stage, pretended to knock him out, and then stood with a foot planted on his chest. All the while she crooned, "Gotta take my chance / Gotta go the distance" before doing a victory dance as fake snow fell snow in celebration of Christmas, and perhaps—this be-

MOLLY BEAUCHEMIN ON "PULL UP TO THE BUMPER"

Grace Jones pioneered the way for Shamir, Stromae, and countless other dance mavericks of today, not just with her bewitching candor, but through her use of androgynous innuendo. 1981's "Pull Up To The Bumper" was initially banned in the United States for suggestive lyrics—"Pull up to my bumper baby/ In your long black limousine"—that were revolutionary because they were smart, risky, and intriguingly gender inclusive, just like Jones herself. By combining Studio 54's pulsing drums and chic new wave licks with the kaleidoscope of Andy Warhol's playhouse (Jones was a regular in both scenes), "Bumper" became a crucial track for American dance music. Its chorus gets under the skin like a percussive, funky itch. Still, lines like "Grease it/ Spray it/ Let me lubricate it" suggest that Jones mastered something years ago that people still crave: songs that push boundaries with their raw sexuality.

SARA BIVIGOU ON THE RUSSELL HARTY INCIDENT

In 1981 Grace Jones pummelled British talk show host Russell Harty live on his namesake BBC show. Harty always sat among the guests on his early evening gabfest and on this particular night he chose to focus his attention on the men to his right, leaving Jones, seated alone to his left, out of much of the conversation. The scene plays out with a frustrated Jones admonishing Harty, "If you turn your back to me one more minute." Harty dismisses her, wagging a finger ("You're going to have another little part of this soon"), before turning away. Jones clips him on the neck and then lands one, two, three more hits in quick succession before slapping him on the head. The confused au-

PHOTO BY JOHN HENSHALL / ALAMY

ing 1979—cocaine. I was hooked.

That jaw-dropping TV appearance prompted a discussion with my high school drama teacher, who bragged that his brother had once met Jones at a Manhattan roller rink. Rather than proffering a business card like one might, she'd handed him a plastic whip emblazoned with her name. I knew at that moment that I belonged in *Grace Jones' New York*; I knew that suburban life would kill me the same way it had killed my alcoholic father. A year later, I arrived.

Jones' "On Your Knees" was the last single I bought before leaving Rochester, and it was one of the first songs I heard on the local disco station upon my arrival in New York City. Subway cars plastered with graffiti bore nearly inscrutable codes I was hungry to crack, for danger preyed upon the ignorant: each weekend brought stories of fellow students who had been mugged. Protesters that summer disrupted the filming of William Friedkin's *Cruising*, which retold the real-life story of a fugitive who'd lured men out of gay bars to bed and then kill them. In that anything-goes, pre-AIDS era at the tail end of the '70s, pleasure and danger were quite literally bedfellows.

That summer of 1979, Studio 54 and symphonic sounds had already peaked; ascendant was the offbeat soul of the much blacker and gayer Paradise Garage, where Jones held her "baby shower"—dressed, according to *Jet*, as a British general. Macho, close-cropped clones ruled the city's mega-discos, but I hadn't escaped my small suburb just to conform in the big city, so I sought out unconventional spaces like Hurrah's, the Mudd Club, and Danceteria, where dub, reggae and post-punk alternated with chilly synth pop and radical funk. All these genres would mingle and mutate in Jones' next incarnation.

When *Muse* fizzled in the clubs and on the charts, Island's Chris Blackwell took over as Jones' producer. "I wanted to treat her not as a model, but to involve her as a musician," he recalls. "Tom Moulton had been recording the instrumentation and then having Grace come in later. I wanted her to feel as though she were a member of a band, and record her the way bands used to make albums, with the singer and the players doing their thing all at once."

Blackwell's approach united two things he knew well: Caribbean ease and British audacity. "I wanted a rhythmic reggae bottom, aggressive rock guitar and atmospheric keyboards in the middle, and Grace on top," he recalls. To get all that, Blackwell assembled a sextet of studio ringers at his Nassau studio, Compass Point. The soon-to-be signature sound of the Compass Point All-Stars went on to animate hits by the Tom Tom Club, Robert Palmer, Joe Cocker, Gwen Guthrie, and others. Blackwell recounts:

I'd been working with Sly [Dunbar] and Robbie [Shakespeare] and Mikey [Chung] and "Sticky" [Uziah Thompson] in Jamaica. They'd played many sessions together, and were already in most aspects a band: I knew they'd generate a groove. Barry Reynolds had just done *Broken English* for me with Marianne Faithful, and Wally Badarou was recommended to me, which was quite fortunate because his contributions worked so well with the others.

The sessions began with an unlikely remake of the Normal's "Warm Leatherette." Jones' version preserves the original's deadpan vocal delivery and minimal melody but drops the tempo to a saunter, twists the rhythm into a sharp funk, and sashays with offhand earnestness, as if sexual intercourse while dying from vehicular collision is just another kink worth trying. The sessions moved with disarming speed and ease: if Grace or the group hadn't nailed a song by the third take, it was dropped and they'd move to the next number.

We'd record a track and then later play it back, and if Grace or the band did something that didn't feel right, we'd just record the whole thing together again very quickly. Grace was inspired by what the band was doing, they were feeding off her, and it was crucial to preserve the purity of their interaction, not mess it up with a lot of adjustments.

Badarou further attests to Jones' active role in the recordings: "Grace was there even during most instrumen-

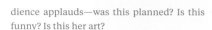

tal overdubbing sessions. She was a part of the sound and the spirit that came out almost from nowhere. We all knew we were in for something unheard before, something quite experimental."

Soon they'd massed enough material for 1980's *Warm Leatherette*: a non-LP B-side, her rendition of Joy Division's "She's Lost Control," and the beginnings of a follow–up LP that would become 1981's *Nightclubbing*. Upon its release, *Leatherette* failed to charm either radio audiences or most dance clubs. It was too authentically reggae for the New Wave crowd, too slow for disco. By the following year, both New York radio and the club scene had grown eclectic. Primed by kindred punk-funk blasts like Yoko Ono's "Walking on Thin Ice" as well as Taana Gardner's "Heartbeat," a far more open-minded dance music world was ready to re-embrace Jones and her new sound.

Early in '81, Jones, Blackwell, Sadkin, and the All-Stars reassembled in Nassau to complete the tracks they'd begun with *Leatherette*, write some new songs, and whip up a few more Blackwell-selected covers.

Nightclubbing would provide Jones with newfound popularity on both sides of the Atlantic. European audiences appreciated "I've Seen That Face Before (Libertango)," a vocal reimagining of Argentine tango master Ástor Piazzolla's 1974 instrumental "Libertango." For that track, Reynolds penned lyrics about a Parisian stalker, and Badarou provided an appropriately haunting introductory riff. Jones lyrics are a rebuttal, *en francais*, penned with the help of Blackwell's girlfriend, actor Nathalie Delon: "What are you looking for? Hoping to find love? Who do you think you are? You hate your life."

In America, Jones's R&B breakthrough came via an instrumental Sly Dunbar side project recorded during the *Warm Leatherette* sessions; it leaked out as "Peanut Butter" on the B-side of kiddie reggae crooner Junior Tucker's "The Kick (Rock On)." Eager to make it hers, Grace co-wrote new lyrics equating cars with carnality. "Pull Up to the Bumper" pushes that metaphor towards lewd entendre: "Grease it, spray it / Let me lubricate it," she drawls. A summertime smash, "Bumper" became one of the last thoroughly sexual jams before a new virus began to complicate that kind of fun.

The sessions for Jones' 1982 record *Living My Life* marked a culmination of the synchronicity between Jones

dience applauds—was this planned? Is this funny? Is this her art?

This was my introduction to the totemic Grace Jones: elegantly beating the hell out of a man who won't take her seriously, her black body and everything it knows asserting itself for the good of fed up women everywhere.

ERIC TORRES ON "BREAKDOWN"

Everyone from Suzi Quatro to the Replacements have covered Tom Petty and the Heartbreakers' 1976 slowburner, "Breakdown", but Grace Jones' take–from 1980's *Warm Leatherette*–is the version most worth discussing. Given a sauntering, reggae reconstruction, Jones' rendering is shaded by a subtle gradation of vocal inflections that give the song a searing potency: she is sturdy and commanding one second, and mournful the next. The song's titular collapse filtered through a distinctly Jonesian lens of fortifying self-sufficiency. Even Petty recognized that quality about Jones, writing a killer kiss-off of a third verse to cap her interpretation: "It's OK if you must go/ I'll understand if you don't/ You say goodbye right now/ I'll still survive somehow/ Why should we let this drag on?" In Jones' more than capable hands, a bluesy classic is transformed into an irresistible clarion call, summoning strength from the depths of its vulnerability.

and the All-Stars. "Blackwell felt the band was so good it deserved to be doing its own material," Badarou remembers. As a result, *Living My Life* is all originals, save for a cover of Melvin Van Peebles' "The Apple Stretching." The rest began with Jones's lyrics, from which Reynolds wrote the music to fit. Recorded in the wake of her breakup with Jean-Paul Goude, the album gets more personal and rigorously percussive: The percolating lead track, "My Jamaican Guy," has been sampled by acts from La Roux to LL Cool J. The title track, "Living My Life," was left off the album but the pointed, ska-punk anthem showcases in stark relief how personal the work was that she was making, a world away from the showtunes and entendres, singing "You kill me for living my life / As much as I can, as black as I am."

ee

By 1982, AIDS and Reaganomics had started striking down Grace's core audience, and the freedoms of the previous decade shifted to contractions. MTV had also arrived, and the New Wave dance sounds it championed—Eurythmics, Culture Club, Duran Duran, and many other sonic stepchildren of the singer—launched a second English invasion on the charts. Jones' singular appearance and meticulously crafted presentation made her a natural fit for the music video, especially in its early, experimental days.

She asserted herself as an astute visual artist at MTV's dawn with her 1982 VHS release, *A One Man Show*. Directed by Goude and nominated in '84 for the first Best Long Form Music Video Grammy, it combines still photography, concert footage, and video clips to distill the pair's simultaneously sensational and intimate collaborations into a heated, unbroken montage. Jones dons pointedly geometric designs that accentuate her angles, clad in screaming Pop Art colors that flash and flatter. Goude's art direction comes alive through Jones, who glares at the camera as if possessed; she's imposing, alien, almighty—it's not surprising that she'd soon would be stealing scenes in *Conan the Destroyer* and *A View to a Kill*.

What came after *One Man* and the Compass Point trilogy would have to top them, and "Slave to the Rhythm" was perhaps the only song that could. Bruce Woolley, co-writer of the Buggles' "Video Killed the Radio Star," wrote it on spec for Frankie Goes to Hollywood, but helped to re-draft it for Jones. Producer Trevor Horn was brought in, and what ensued was a nine-month studio odyssey that would allegedly cost Island $385,000, a fortune for a singer who had never scaled the US pop charts. The exorbitant single was offset by padding the album with eight different versions of "Slave to the Rhythm" in attempt to break even.

"I remember a huge amount of experimentation with early digital techniques, the Synclavier, Sony digital tape spliced with sticky tape, and the Fairlight," Woolley recalls. "We recorded eight different versions, about one every four weeks, with Horn and Blackwell in search of the perfect track." Between her acting roles, Jones was returning to the studio month after month, to update her vocals on the latest arrangements and versions. She'd just signed a massive deal with EMI subsidiary Manhattan Records in the United States, and her new label assumed that all this activity meant another Island album. Woolley alleges that EMI were on the verge of suing Blackwell, but incredibly everyone agreed to co-release the album on Island/Manhattan Records.

"Slave to the Rhythm" was finally released in October 1985, and one would be hard-pressed to argue that all the laborious studio work and astronomical expenditures weren't justified: Horn's production work is ornate and opulent, lurid and symphonic. The spell cast by a larger-than-life black woman singing both metaphorically and directly about slavery is profound; the lyrics coax infinite interpretations. *The Face*—England's authority on all things hip—declared "Slave" *the* single of 1985, and Jones appeared on the magazine's January '86 cover pointedly painted in whiteface. From the pure gloss of its ambition to the obsessiveness of its lyric, "Slave" *is* the '80s.

Her ultimate hit in much of the world, the sheer enormity "Slave" underscores Jones' incandescence and charisma made her bigger than her sales figures indicate. Yet, MTV virtually ignored "Slave" and it's Goude-directed video. Even when framed by Horn's familiar transatlantic brilliance, Jones was, for them, still too black, too strong. Nevertheless, she got over elsewhere on the sheer magnitude of her presence. With the help of Hollywood and

some crazy commercials for Citroën, Honda Scooters, and Sun Country Wine Coolers, she became more massive than ever.

"I like conflicts," she told *Playboy* in 1985. "I love competition. I like discovering things for myself. It's a childlike characteristic, actually. But that gives you a certain amount of power, and people are intimidated by that."

With Goude and Blackwell out of the picture, Jones wanted more involvement for her debut album for Manhattan, 1986's *Inside Story*. Taking EMI A&R head Bruce Garfield's direction to "imagine a leaf being blown through the streets of New York, twisting and turning in the sunshine" as a starting point, Jones and Woolley wrote every song together, then joined multi-platinum Svengali Nile Rodgers in New York to transform their demos. This mutually flattering union would yield her last R&B radio victory, "I'm Not Perfect (But I'm Perfect for You)." Indicting white-collar criminals and Hollywood liars, *Inside Story* reveals the singer's observant, socially conscious side, while the jagged arrangements mesh Rodgers' ricocheting, jazz-schooled guitar with Woolley's smart pop. It's a singer-songwriter record you can dance to.

She followed it with 1989's *Bulletproof Heart* which yielded one resplendent club triumph, "Love on Top of Love," courtesy of David Cole & Robert Clivillés, a house remix/production duo who'd soon score with their C+C Music Factory. Jones co-wrote and co-produced most of the rest with her new husband Chris Stanley, whose output fell far below her avant standards; the two soon divorced. Having tried harder, thought broader, and crossed more boundaries than most of her contemporaries, this dance-floor renegade closed out the decade boxed in and coasting.

T. COLE RACHEL ON VAMP

Grace Jones fascinated me at a pretty young age (seeing her as a kid while watching *Conan The Destroyer* with my dad both scared and excited me), but I didn't become legitimately obsessed with her until seeing the movie *Vamp* at a sleepover in 1986. In the film Jones plays Queen Katrina, a wicked vampiress running a strip club somewhere in Kansas (naturally). She makes her first on-screen appearance nude, save for a red bob wig and full body paint, doing a seductive dance that is as patently bizarre as it is weirdly erotic. At the time I didn't really know much about her music (I was eleven years old and lived on a farm), nor could I appreciate the fact that she was dressed for the film by Azzedine Alaïa and Issey Miyake, or that her body paint and the chair upon which she writhes were done by Keith Haring. The film is glorious '80s trash of the highest order, but Jones manages to transform the whole thing into high art by virtue of simply being there and (even though she's playing the undead) just being herself—beautiful, artful, exotic, and frighteningly wild.

By the late '80s, I had moved to San Francisco; AIDS was decimating the gay community. One night in 1993, I finally got my chance to see Jones perform at a local gay night club. I took my friend Brian, whose partner Mark was too sick to join us. Jones' lived up to her reputation for diva behavior, and didn't take the stage until well after midnight. At first she stuck to her hits, including that year's house excursion "Sex Drive." But it soon became apparent that she didn't need the spectacular filigree of her Goude years. The special effect was her smile: It just wouldn't stop, and soon it became contagious—Jones positively beamed, giddy. And she didn't back away from that elephant in the room: she dedicated one song to the late Keith Haring, who'd used her body for a canvas on the occasion of her legendary 1985 Paradise Garage performance.

That night's show was remarkable for the simple fact that Jones just kept on going, granting one encore request after the other, waiting patiently while the soundman scoured her backing tapes to find her fans' offbeat choices. When she got to such minor numbers as "Crush," it became clear that she didn't want to leave. She was giving as much of herself as she could to the beleaguered troops, knowing full well that many wouldn't live long enough to see her again. A few months after that show, I inherited Mark's cherished copy of Goude's memoir/Grace Jones art book *Jungle Fever*; he and Brian died within weeks of each other.

Jones' lust for life that night represented not just resilience to repression, but also a way of fighting back, one that sent this message: we, who are thought less than, shall burn brighter than our oppressors. That was why she was so beloved: because she led the way, even when we couldn't proceed. Along with the lesbians and lucky survivors who nursed our fallen, Jones had borne witness to what Reagan, Bush, and most of the country willfully ignored; she knew the toll of it all.

Throughout the '90s, rumors of new albums surfaced: Blackwell recorded several sessions, so did Tricky. Even Moulton buried the hatchet for a benefit single, a 1997 house remake of Candi Staton's "Victim." But Island nixed its release on conceptual grounds: they thought Grace Jones couldn't be a victim of anything.

In 2008, Jones unexpectedly reemerged with *Hurricane*, her first record in 19 years. She'd not only brought back Woolley and the Compass Point All-Stars, but also added contributors like Emmy-winning composers Wendy Melvoin and Lisa Coleman, who worked with her for a month in their home on "Williams' Blood." Roof-raising yet lyrically contemplative, the gospel-shaded canticle revisits the pressures of growing up with politicians on one side of the family tree and Puritans on the other.

"Prince has a presence and everybody in the room goes, 'Woah,'" Melvoin attests from first-hand knowledge: she and Coleman were key members of his *Purple Rain*–era backing band, the Revolution. "When Grace walks into the room, it's more subtle, but it has the same effect. You just go, 'My God, she's taken up all of the space with that personality.'"

Hurricane mirrors that kaleidoscope. Unlike commonplace pop and rock luminaries who take extended vacations, Jones came back more polished and unpredictable than ever. With her trenchant track "Corporate Cannibal," she even protests capitalist dehumanization by embodying it via grinding, insidious metal. But while her image as a constantly morphing, couture-clad hellion persists, the sixty-seven-year-old iconoclast stays true to herself. After all these years and so many disciples, there's still no one like her.

While gathering up my Grace Jones memories, I was reminded of what Sonic Youth's Kim Gordon said about entertainers. This was 25 years ago, so my memory may have altered her words, but it goes something like this: *We pay to bask in the confidence of our most beloved performers so that we may learn to similarly love ourselves.* Grace did that for me, and for her audience, for anyone who has ever been too queer, too black, too female, or too freaky for the world around them. Grace Jones is liberation.

BARRY WALTERS *has been writing about pop music for the past thirty years.*

PHOTO COURTESY OF DAILY MAIL / REX / ALAMY

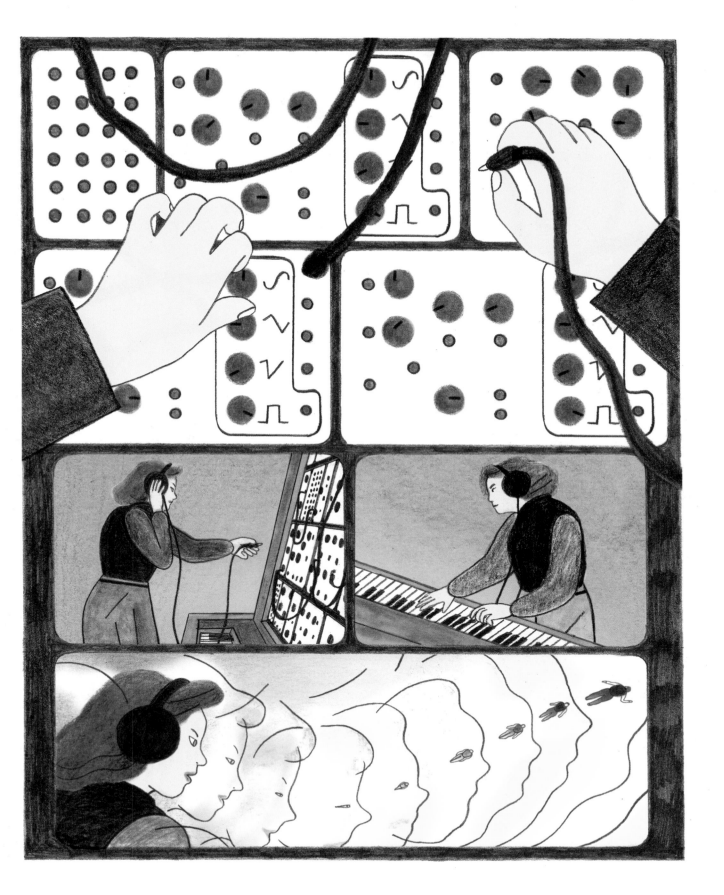

PITCHFORK *TOONS* • SARA DRAKE

12 OUNCES OF PURE GOLD

The Champagne of Beers

#IAmRich

Miller
HIGH LIFE

Miller® HIGH LIFE
ESTD ★ 1903
The Champagne of Beers
12 FLUID OUNCES (.355 LITERS)

A
Conversation
with
Terry Riley

BY PETER MARGASAK

ILLUSTRATIONS BY LOUISE POMEROY

Terry Riley turns eighty on June 24 of this year, and celebrations have been taking place all over the globe to mark the birthday of this singular composer, musician, and thinker. Along with La Monte Young, Steve Reich, and Philip Glass, Riley is widely acknowledged as one of the key architects of minimalism, a style he more or less dismisses. His work over the last five decades has been hugely influential upon such a wide swath of musicians that it's impossible and foolish to reduce it to a single discipline. Riley's importance in the development of tape music, improvisation, string quartet, New Age, electronic music, and, yes, minimalism is arguably greater than that of any of his minimalist cohorts, and he continues to relish the craft of music-making, collaboration, and experimentation.

Riley found common cause with Young in the late '50s while both were studying music at UC Berkeley, but it took another half-decade for Riley to begin finding his voice—most famously with his 1964 masterpiece "In C," which continues to be one of the most widely performed experimental works of the 20th century. Although he began creating unabashedly experimental composition as a student, over his career he incorporated a deep appreciation for—as well as a rigorous study of—improvisation and Indian classical music (he was a disciple of Pandit Pran Nath for over two decades) into his work.

I spoke with Riley in late March in Knoxville, Tennessee, where he was performing at the Big Ears Festival. He played an improvised set on piano with guitarist Gyan Riley (his son), and violinist Tracy Silverman. He also participated in a concert by Kronos Quartet, which performed their 2004 commission Cusp of Magic with pipa master Wu Man. As part of an encore, Riley joined Kronos and Laurie Anderson for "Jam in D."

For most of the '70s, Riley gave largely improvised solo concerts for organ and electronics, but toward the end of the decade he developed a friendship with David Harrington of the Kronos Quartet, when both were teaching at Oakland's Mills College. Eventually Harrington convinced him to write a string quartet for the group, although Riley hadn't written any serious notated music in a decade.

Since 1980, Riley has composed an unprecedented twenty-seven works for Kronos, a sustained collaboration that led to more commissions of notated work for the composer and altered his career trajectory, which now balances his improvisational impulses with his skill for standard notation. On June 16, Nonesuch Record will release *Sunrise of the Planetary Dream Collector*, a five-CD box set celebrating the Kronos/Riley partnership, which will include "One Earth, One People, One Love," a movement from the as-yet-unreleased 2001 multimedia project, *Sun Rings*.

You seem to take it in stride that your work has often existed in a kind of no-man's land between distinct styles or genres. Were you frustrated early on when people wanted to pin you one way or another?

It was hard in a way because we were struggling with our own ideas and concepts, but I was getting a lot of feedback from friends and audiences even in those days. The small groups I was playing for—there was something exciting to them. That helps a lot, when you know you're not out here in the dark. La Monte doesn't care if one person in the world gets it because he's got his vision and he's very singular about his approach to this work, but I was curious if what I was doing was going to work, so the feedback helped me to continue, to forge my way ahead.

When I was in Europe I was still struggling to find out just where I was going to go. I was there for about two years, working as a cabaret piano player, accompanying floor-show acts all around France. I had a little notebook where I would keep musical ideas, but they weren't going anywhere, they were just collecting and I wasn't composing. I didn't really feel like composing. I wanted to travel around Europe and drink it in for a couple of years.

It wasn't until I was getting reading to come back that I ran into Chet Baker and Ken Dewey, who wanted to do this theater piece called *The Gift*. Baker was in Paris, had just gotten out of jail, and he was playing with a quartet. We approached him and said yeah, we'll do it. I recorded him and cut up a lot of loops of stuff he was playing and ran it through processing at the studios of Radio France—this was still in the days of mono—and I developed this thing of stringing the tape across two tape recorders and the long, looping delays. That's when I started thinking, "Okay, there's a whole universe of possibilities here, all of these cycling planets of musical notes that make a kind of form." At the time I think I got a vision of what I was going to do for the rest of my life.

The Gift was definitely a turning point for me. I got very excited by that project. When I came back I was so totally broke I couldn't even buy a tape recorder, but I did eventually manage to get one and I started experimenting with tape loops again and started writing little pieces. I was asked to do a one-man show at the San Francisco Tape Music Center in 1964. By then I had collected enough stuff

to do it show. I'd also written "In C" by that point.

It seems that you've always rejected any sort of hierarchical view of different sorts of music—

Lou Harrison said once, when he hears something he says, "Me too." You don't feel separate from what you're hearing, and eventually—it doesn't mean you do everything you hear, but it's all in there and you're just a mixing pot. There's always the accusation that you're collecting from here and there, but I don't see it that way. I see it all as training. These things have to interact some way, and they become who you are.

The body of work you've created with Kronos Quartet is not only remarkable in its size and breadth, but it's also unprecedented that a composer and an ensemble have worked so prolifically together. When David Harrington first convinced you to compose for them, did you foresee this kind of relationship developing?

Neither of us could. But I immediately felt some kind of great connection with David, so we've just kept it going. It's gotten better over the years. I'll just about finish a project and he'll call me up and say, "I've got this great idea." It's kind of been that way over the years.

Has it usually been him coming to you with specific ideas for a piece?

It's usually a very open proposal, but sometimes it can be something like the NASA project, *Sun Rings*, which was quite involved in the preparation. We took a trip down to Cape Kennedy and watched a launch, we took a tour of the whole premises, went to Iowa to meet Don Gurnett—so it was kind of a long buildup for a piece like that. Sometimes the preparations are very involved because we really want to make sure we're on the same page about how we're viewing the project. We don't always think the same way at the beginning, but we keep in touch about it.

You hadn't been writing notated works for a quite a while when David approached you. Were you hesitant at first—like, *Doesn't he know I don't really do that?*

Well, he had been checking my music out. He obviously

knew that I *could* do it. I had written a string quartet in college—in 1960 I wrote a quartet and a string trio. I have really liked string quartet forms my whole life. I fell in love, one period, with Bartok quartets, as most composers do, because it was such a great testament to that form. I felt I could write it. If that been piccolo and harp, it might've been different.

I was one of the two people who auditioned their tape that they sent down from Seattle when they were applying to be in residence at Mills College, and when I heard the tape I was really excited by it. They were playing new music in a really energetic and exciting way—much like they are today. They already had it back then.

You've usually worked pretty closely with them in developing each piece, right? It's not as if you just

send off the manuscript and then they play it.

It's been different with each project. For *Sun Rings* we had quite a few sessions before the piece was finished. I was doing my own publishing, so it was easy for me to go down there, print out a few pages, and show them that so they had an idea what I had in mind for the piece.

I've read that occasionally they'll interpret something you've written differently than what you had in mind. o you enjoy those surprises?

Oh, yeah. I like to be surprised, with my own performances as well. For me, that's what makes music really alive, that things come up that you don't expect. Kronos is very good at seeing deep into the material and seeing possibilities. Their rehearsals are very interesting—it's like four people having a conversation. David directs it, like a moderator, and most of the ideas flow out of that first chair. There is a really good interchange between the musicians—they check each other. They're very good at accepting criticism from each other and considering it, and then doing it all again. I must say I've never sat in on a session where any attitude comes out, and I've been at hundreds of them. It's very professional and it's all about the work.

What has marked the most successful collaborations for you?

The ones where you get to spend more time, to go deep, seem to be the most valuable. Occasionally I'll have a single meeting on the stage with somebody and it will be thrilling for everybody. But usually it's the ones that develop over years and you start understanding each other and how you do things. When you're playing you don't feel like two different people—one mind is controlling everything. That's the ideal for me because it takes everything up to another level of intuition. It happens a lot with musicians I play with in small ensembles. I play a lot with my son Gyan, and that's probably the most intuitive relationship I have with another musician.

Do you think you would have written so many other notated works over the last four and a half decades without the Kronos connection?

No, it definitely was a turn in the road. I was going one way for many years, playing these solo organ concerts, and later on with synthesizers and voice, but they were essentially improvised concerts. I didn't see any reason to write it down because I was the only one doing it. Once people heard the stuff I was writing for Kronos, other groups started approaching me.

Since you've written so many notated works over the last few decades, do you have to compartmentalize those ideas? I assume you improvise when you're writing, but I wonder if there's much bleed between the two?

That's a really good question. I've trained as an Indian classical musician since 1970, and one of the big processes of Indian classical music is you take a phrase and just turn it inside out. It's a simple concept from the beginning—you

have a mode and a rhythmic structure—but out of that you have to develop a really fertile imagination or else it gets boring right away. When I hear a musical phrase—when I wake up at night or from dreams—I'm working out variations on themes. It's always in my head, some kind of variational process, or what that particular melody might generate later on. That's really the basis of my writing. It's kind of a mental exercise, gymnastics with musical ideas, combining them, permuting them. There is that improvisational element going into the flow of the written notation.

Do you find it frustrating to finalize a project with a notated score—that you can't keep searching for additional permutations or developments? Did you have to get used to something being complete? Because there are infinite possibilities with improvisation.

A lot of pieces I have gone back to over the years and changed them. Stravinsky and most composers have pieces they're not satisfied with, so that's an option. Now I have a publisher and they can get a little frustrated when you keep sending in revisions. But yeah, it's always going on. I'll think of new ideas for a piece and I'll either start a new work because it has enough change that it can stand on its own, or I'll put it in as a revision later. Music is a continuum; there's absolutely no stopping point.

In your work with La Monte Young and the Theatre of Eternal Music there was a drift away from notated music, and a rejection of the idea that there was a definitive way of playing a piece—also, that the performer could be the composer...

That was a really big change in contemporary music. There might've been a band that came along earlier, but the Theatre of Eternal Music was one of the places where a composer gathered other people around him to perform his work mostly because he couldn't find anybody who would understand the work to perform it well. That situation was a lot different in the '50s and '60s when I was beginning to write—it really was hard to find performers who would understand what you were doing, so you'd end up playing it yourself. When La Monte and I were going to school, we used to play a lot of four-handed piano on two pianos. We improvised a lot because we both understood what we were doing. The categories about how much is composed, how much is improvised—it's just what you do.

You studied Indian classical music with Pandit Pran Nath for many years, and you have had longstanding interest in North African music. Is it a challenge to work with an instrument from a foreign culture or to work in a tradition you don't know fluently?

Evan Zipporyn has a gamelan at MIT and he asked me to write a piece for it. So I approached it by just writing a piece kind of like I would write for Western instruments, but I knew the tuning of the gamelan, so I re-tuned my synthesizer in something close to what the gamelan was. Of course, gamelan tunings aren't precise like Indian classical music—it's like a third of a tone lower or something like that, and all gamelans have different tunings—but every builder constructs to his own ear. That was another thing: How do you know what you're gonna hear?

With Wu Man it was a little different. We had some sessions together, one on one, before I wrote the piece. We hung out and I sang some raga scales to her to see how that kind of inflection would sound on the pipa. Then I noticed in the Chinese music this beautiful kind of parallel system that wasn't like raga, but it was so colorful, the way she could bend notes and ornament. Having that in my ear, I kind of wrote general directions for her and then worked with her in rehearsals if something didn't quite sound right. She has a really good sense of how to make a line sound.

There were a lot of things that were probably awkward to play on a pipa, but she's such a consummate musician, she just takes the challenge. You look for guidance from the performer. I like a performer to be able to play the music as if they wrote it, they feel it, like, *This is my own, I own this*. You try to write something you feel that they'll really get excited about playing and then let them find a real particular way of playing it. As long as I've written for guitar—and my son Gyan is a great guitarist—I still can't write idiomatic guitar music because I don't play it, and I'll probably never get there. But working with him over the years, I'll try something and he'll go through it all and then say, "Dad, it would sound a little better if I do it like this." I like working like that. As a performer myself, I feel that if I don't own the music, I'm just a kind of an office clerk or something.

You emerged at a time when there was limited access to such music, and I'm assuming a lot of your learning was intuitive and self-driven. Has your approach to incorporating or working with non-Western musical traditions changed over the years as the access has increased?

When I actually started hearing authentic music from Morocco—we were living in Algeciras in Spain, which is a little fishing village across from Ceuta—I would listen to Radio Ceuta all night smoking ganja. We visited Morocco and went to cafés and would hear these families playing music—an old grandfather playing something with a ten-year old, and the father of the ten-year old, and they would sit around the house and just play music. At that time I had been starting to write pieces like Stockhausen. No, that wasn't the way I wanted to go. I didn't want it to be this intellectual thing, I wanted it to come from a kind of feeling. Although I didn't belong to a family tradition, that's what I was attracted to.

That eventually led me to India because that's where the families learn together, and genetically, after about twenty generations of musicians, these kids come out masters when they're three years old. I traveled around Europe for two years and I had two LPs with me: one was *Cookin' With the Miles Davis Quartet* and the other was Moroccan music from the Atlas Mountains. I carried them with me, and whenever I'd be somewhere where there was a turntable, I'd throw them on and listen for hours. I was really interested in Miles Davis and modal, long improvisations, and of course I had heard Coltrane by that time and Ornette Coleman, but I didn't feel like where I was necessarily going to end up.

I had been playing jazz with a rehearsal band in San Francisco in 1964 and 1965, and I wrote this piece called "Tread on the Trail," which was this out piece that I was thinking could be played by jazz musicians. It was a little bit like "In C," written all on one page. I was headed that way, the way of some long modal improvisational ideas that were spiritually oriented.

When you were working with tape or electronic keyboards or developing other things like the time-lag accumulator, you had to be inventive and progress through trial and error. Obviously technology has evolved at breakneck pace in regard to such things, but I wonder if you think it's too easy now, in a way. Working the way you did back then

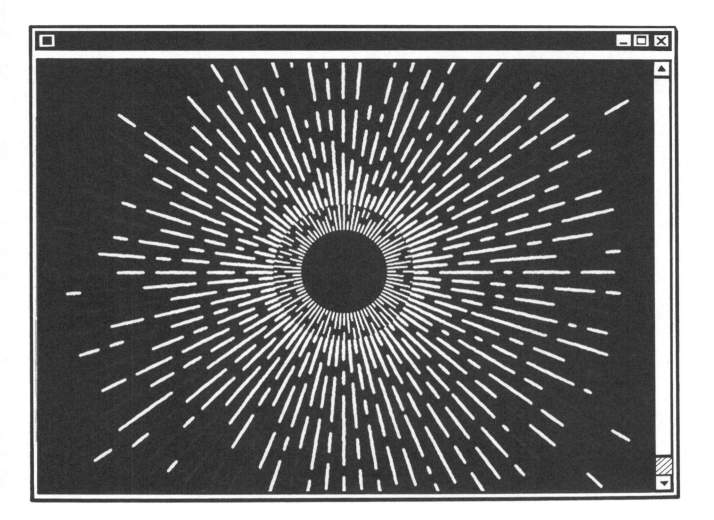

must've forced you to really become intimate with how everything worked. Things are so easy now that one doesn't necessarily need to understand how these things work.

I don't use any of that stuff anymore, so that kind of answers your question. It was exciting when it was new. If I'd miraculously had some of this technology in those days, I would've been blown away. I'm sure anyone would have been. I was using tape delays in live performance with my keyboards, and I remember talking with Chet Wood, who was my technician who would travel with me, about memory—"Can I get a longer tape delay than one-one-a-half seconds?" And he'd say, "Oh, that's going to be way in the future." It just seemed unfathomable that you could have memory stored like that and actually do clean digital sound.

Around 1977 we bought an old Bombardier computer from Don Buchla and Chet built the first digital delay for me— there were already some built but I couldn't afford them. It was cheaper for me to pay him to come and work and put this computer together. I helped him solder stuff and we got the thing working. Things like that, no matter how good some expensive thing is, there's something about building something from the ground up and the excitement of it actually working for the first time. I know now that with an iPhone I can play a whole concert. I've got a synthesizer I've worked with for about a 15 years—a Korg Trident, which is a really good sampling synthesizer. I like to take one instrument and really go deep into it, really get to know it. It's not cutting-edge technology at all.

When working with tapes, like on *The Gift*—wasn't that integral in opening things up? Do you think it

Terry Riley
Beverly Hills, 1993

would've been the same if you had been working with a computer?

You're dealing with really elemental processes. Sometimes I was using chance techniques, blindly cutting a piece of tape without knowing what was on it, but it was really interesting to put those on and listen to them, and they would create a rhythm that you could use later, write

something out, or have someone play something to that rhythm. Now there's so much technology that you don't know where to begin. I'm not really interested in technology for me. I loved it during the period when I was in it, but now my challenges and wishes are more scaled down, more about ordinary musical processes.

You once seemed unconcerned with documenting

or recording your work, as you focused more on creating than preserving. But that seems to have changed, first with Gary Todd and the Cortical Foundation and then with the work carried on with Tom Welsh and Elision Fields in reissuing or preserving unissued recordings. Are you happy that that material is available now?

I was surprised. I worked with such primitive equipment there's always tons of 60-cycle hum, which is compounded by all the [degradation] of all the loops and delays. But then the noise music movement happened. Part of what I liked about it was that there was a new group of people who liked this kind of otherworldly, primitive, grinding stuff on the early tape pieces. I loved it, but when I made my piece "The Bird of Paradise" I thought nobody was going to like it, because it's kind of like a wormhole grinding away at your brain. It sat in my barn for years, deteriorating.

Gary Todd came up and rescued a lot of that stuff. At one point I was going to take all those tapes to the dump; I told my wife Anne, "We're not going to do anything with these old tapes," and she talked me out of it. Gary took them all down to LA and he digitized them. I see the value of them now. I always liked my piece "You're Nogood," which I always thought was a pretty cool concept, and it was one of the cleaner pieces. Something like that I was planning to hang on to, although many did get lost, just from moving around. But enough got saved that people could see I was doing that work at the time. Life's for the living, and when I'm not around anymore I'm certainly not going to care about that old stuff. I work harder now than I ever did.

How does it feel when a piece like "In C" is not only viewed as such a game-changer and influential piece, but that it feels alive in a way that few compositions from that era still do—that it keeps engaging new audiences and new musicians who feel the freedom to put their own personality into it? There's that recording of it performed by Malian musicians, which seems to make inherent connections between your own ideas and local traditions.

What I like about it is the fact that it kind of brings communities of musicians together. Hearing the Mali thing that Andre de Ridder and Brian Eno did really made me happy, because I keep telling people, "It's been done

enough now that you can feel free to look for new ways to do it," although some people still want to do it like the 1968 recording on CBS. There's so many thousands of performances of that piece, and it does seem to bring a lot of joy to the musicians playing it and to the audiences. Maybe it's the C major–ish optimism and a kind of ritual of happy people somewhere in the future. Not here on Planet Earth!

I don't know how that happened. I didn't think a lot about that piece—it's one I just wrote, it just came to me. But sometimes that's the best way. It was very exciting when it first came to me. I didn't know how to perform it. The original performance took place at the Tape Music Center with Pauline [Oliveros], Ramon [Sender], Steve [Reich], John Gibson—about 15 people altogether—but the recording that came out on CBS was from the group I was working with up in Buffalo, the Creative Associates under Lukas Foss.

For the Malian piece, Andre was going down there to Africa for some other projects with Africa Express and he just happened to have the score for "In C" tucked in his suitcase. They were doing something else and they were looking for other things to try and he said, "Why don't we try this?" It just kind of happened. The Malian musicians didn't read music, so he taught it to them all. Then some of them said, "I like that, but I'd rather do it this way," and he let them, probably a more traditional way of looking at rhythm.

When we did the the 45th anniversary performance at Carnegie Hall that David Harrington organized—that was the most spectacular concert I had ever been to, of anything. It was sold out, a two-hour performance of "In C," and David had gotten together all these different people and groups: 65 musicians, a children's choir, Joan La Barbara, Morton Subotnick, Phil Glass. It was like superstars on the stage, and we played for two hours, and at the end the entire Carnegie Hall stood up. We were blown away— we didn't even know if anyone was still in the audience because we were so into the performance. I can't perform it again after that. ✐

PETER MARGASAK *has been a staff music writer at the* Chicago Reader *since 1995 and is a regular contributor to* Downbeat.

TEN ESSENTIAL TERRY RILEY RECORDINGS

Music for the Gift (ELISION FIELDS)

This essential archival release compiles Riley's most important early tape pieces, including radical manipulations of live jazz performed by a Chet Baker–led quintet (*Music for the Gift*) and snippets of "Shotgun" by Booker T and the MGs (*Bird of Paradise*). Together these works seem to anticipate the experimental turntablism and sampling of Christian Marclay (albeit practiced on a different medium), where prerecorded materials are utterly transformed into something new. "Mescalin Mix" is the earliest of his surviving tape pieces, a spooky, appropriately psychedelic collision of warped, manipulating voices and underwater piano made in San Francisco before his European travels. The collection also includes a 1960 recording of his "Concert for Two Pianos and Five Tape Recorders," performed by Riley and La Monte Young on prepared pianos with five tape recorders adding grinding, dissonant musique concrete–style sounds.

In C (SONY CLASSICAL)

The first recording of this landmark piece was made in New York in 1968 with members of the Creative Associates, a loose group of forward-looking players directed by Lukas Foss and based at SUNY Buffalo. Although most versions of the work eventually featured 20 or more musicians, this version used only 10, including trumpeter Jon Hassell, trombonist (and future Pauline Oliveros collaborator) Stuart Dempster, and percussionist Jan Williams. The single-page score, written in 1964 for an indefinite number of performers using any instrumentation, features 53 short phrases to be played sequentially for any duration (although some may bypassed), with the typical performance lasting between 45 and 90 minutes. This minimalist classic has taken on a life of its own (see below), but this is the recording that established it as a standard.

Reed Streams (ELISION FIELDS)

The early fruits of Riley's experimentation with tape loops turned up on this self-released 1966 album on two hard-hitting pieces: one performed on a rickety harmonium ("Untitled Organ") and the other on soprano saxophone ("Dorian Streams"). Both feature short, repeating four- and eight-note phrases that morph slowly, but their power comes from clouds of overtones created by the live tape loops. The CD reissue adds a weird version of "In C" called "Mantra," performed by the French-Canadian large band L'Infonie, directed by Walter Boudreau. The ensemble misread Riley's score and played a series of three eight-notes from the score as triplets, mauling the original instructions but delivering something wonderfully ragged and trippy.

You're No Good (CORTICAL FOUNDATION)

Unfortunately out of print due to licensing issues, this remarkable collection includes the 1967 title track, a tape piece that combined harsh, proto-industrial sine-wave tones and wildly diced-and-sliced manipulations of an R&B song by the Harvey Arverne Dozen. At the time Riley had taken to calling himself Poppy Nogood, after a phrase used by his daughter, so he was attracted to the tune, the title of which he retained for the piece. Riley referred to it as a "a set of variations," and indeed he puts it through the ringer: His treatment was done for a Philadelphia nightclub, and it stands as a crazed, experimental disco remix. The second disc features an inspired 62-minute excerpt of his Indian-derived "Poppy Nogood" from an all-night concert, also in Philadelphia, that features endless permutations of his soprano saxophone treated by his tape-loop system he called the "time-lag accumulator."

A Rainbow in Curved Air (SONY)

Sometimes it seems to damn Riley to attribute things that seem clearly influenced by his work, and this late-'60s masterpiece clobbered the Who (who namechecked the composer on their 1971 hit "Baba O'Riley," which swiped the swirling electric arpeggios that open the tune from him), Mike Oldfield, Tangerine Dream, and an endless proliferation of New Age musicians. The rapidly pulsing figures played on electric organ, electric harpsichord, soprano saxophone, and percussion—all overdubbed and sped up on tape by Riley—maintain a hypnotic power and beauty decades later that obliterates all comers. It's hard to imagine techno and ambient music without him, although I would never hold him responsible for those.

Church of Anthrax (WOUNDED BIRD)

Something of an outlier in Riley's vast discography, this 1971 collaboration with John Cale, whom he met working with La Monte Young's Theatre of Eternal Music in the early '60s, nevertheless demonstrates Riley's open-mindedness and the fluidity of his ideas in a rock music context. His piano, organ, and saxophone improvisations ripple, surge, and float through tough, loping grooves and pretty balladry sketched out by his partner, whose production job clearly privileged his own contributions.

Shri Camel (CBS)

An ideal iteration of the largely improvised organ pieces Riley performed all over the world, especially in Europe, during the 1970s, using electric keyboards and looping delays—this one using just intonation—*Shri Camel* (1980) is the satisfying, full-formed end game of the various "Dervishes" pieces he played earlier in the decade.

Chanting the Light of Foresight (NEW ALBION)

Written for the singular Bay Area saxophone quartet ROVA, this 1991 work found Riley's improvisational ethos reversed when paired with the musicians themselves, who rarely played completely notated music. The reedists ended up writing "The Chord of War," one of six movements, based on ideas presented by Riley, for a furious battle sequence, but otherwise they bring a meditative serenity, rich in overtones, to the composer's stately writing.

The Cusp of Magic (NONESUCH)

One of Riley's strongest works for Kronos Quartet, this 2004 piece includes the twangy Chinese pipa played by virtuoso Wu Man, with further enhancements including subtle synthesizer washes, ritualistic drum beats (played by violinist David Harrington's foot), and sounds from various musical toys collected by the string quartet from around the globe. The six-movement work draws upon rites from Native American, Indian, and even Cuban traditions, marked by passages of stark meditation and thick, driving rhythms, with the composer writing heavy, viscous passages for the strings.

Africa Express Presents...Terry Riley In C in Mali
(TRANSGRESSIVE)

Riley's "In C" has been performed thousands of times over the last five-plus decades, and there are dozens and dozens of recordings, including takes by Bang on a Can All-Stars, Acid Mothers Temple & Melting Paraiso U.F.O., Portishead guitarist Adrian Utley, and Cleveland proto-punks the Styrenes, among many others. But this recent version recorded in Mali under the direction of conductor Andre de Ridder, with Damon Albarn, Nick Zinner, and Brian Eno joining a slew of traditional musicians, not only brings a radically different complexion to the piece, but also demonstrates its versatility and adaptability.

Jelly Rolls & Candy Lickers

A Brief History of Cunnilingus in Black Pop Music

BY ELIJAH WALD

ILLUSTRATIONS BY HANNAH K. LEE

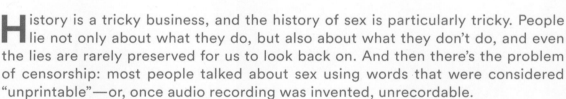

H istory is a tricky business, and the history of sex is particularly tricky. People lie not only about what they do, but also about what they don't do, and even the lies are rarely preserved for us to look back on. And then there's the problem of censorship: most people talked about sex using words that were considered "unprintable"—or, once audio recording was invented, unrecordable.

Fortunately, a few artists and styles pushed the boundaries, and in the early twentieth century, African American blues singers led that push. Blues was considered low-down, honky-tonk music, performed for audiences of gamblers, prostitutes, and laborers. Most lyrics were still censored in print or on record, but a handful of examples have survived to suggest what was lost. For example, Jelly Roll Morton recorded a long, uncensored session for the Library of Congress in 1938, in which he demonstrated the sort of material he performed in New Orleans whorehouses shortly after the turn of the century. One of those verses, in his theme song, "Winin' Boy Blues," went like this:

> Dime's worth of beefsteak, and a nickel's worth of lard.
> Get a dime's worth of beefsteak, and a nickel's worth of lard.
> Yes, a dime's worth of beefsteak, nickel's worth of lard,
> I'll salivate your pussy till my peter get hard,
> I'm the winin' boy, don't deny my name.

At the turn of the twentieth century no one was writing about cunnilingus, except in medical texts and under-the-counter porn, but in 1926 Theodore van de Velde published one of the first modern sex manuals, *Ideal Marriage*, and his take on oral sex neatly recapitulated Morton's blues verse:

> The most simple and obvious substitute for the inadequate lubricant is the natural moisture of the salivary glands…. This may best, most appropriately, and most expeditiously be done without the intermediary offices of the fingers, but through what I prefer to term the kiss of genital stimulation or genital kiss: by gentle and soothing caresses with lips and tongue.

He added in a footnote that he was avoiding the technical term cunnilingus, because it was used to "refer to pathological practices," while "I treat of manifestations which are, in their present context, absolutely unobjectionable and legitimate."

Legitimate as such manifestations might be, both Morton and Van de Velde presented them from a strictly male point of view, as lubricating foreplay before the main event—indeed, Van de Velde argued that pursuing oral sex to the point of orgasm was pathological.

Tellingly, the only other early version I have found of Morton's verse shifted the theme away from oral sex: a lyric in the Library of Congress, apparently collected in the 1910s, starts the same way, but finishes: "I'll Vaseline your coozie till my cock gets hard."

That variant was apparently collected from white sources, which is particularly relevant because by the later twentieth century there was a widespread stereotype in black culture that eating pussy is a white thing—when I was in high school, it was something black guys teased white guys about. And that brings us to another disconnect between Afro- and Euro-American societies. In white culture the word "cock" is used for penis, and "cocksucker" is typically glossed as a homophobic slur, but in black culture, especially in the South, that word was consistently used to mean vulva—it still turns up with that meaning in southern rap lyrics. The African American sociolinguist Geneva Smitherman defines it in her dictionary of black slang as: "A man who is weak, passive, emasculated. Derived from the notion that a man who performs oral sex on a woman is a weakling." And she adds, "the myth is that African American men don't go down on women."

Given that myth, it is interesting that there are so many lyrics in black culture about men doing exactly that, and virtually none in white culture. One reason may be the audience: in white culture, "dirty" songs and verses have typically been recited in all-male environments, as adolescent naughtiness, but blues was always sung for a largely female audience—albeit at times a female audience of sex workers in red light districts catering to semi-adolescent white males.

One could argue that since "cocksucker" is an insult, African Americans clearly disapproved of the act, but that argument is complicated: one of the ways historians demonstrate the existence of illicit acts is prohibitions against them—like, there usually isn't a lot of energy expended on attacking a behavior unless a lot of people are doing it.

In any case, Smitherman's gloss fits one of the ongoing themes in many of the lyrics, which is that men don't like to do it. There are a couple of other themes that surface alongside that, though—like, that women do like it, and that men had better be aware of the fact. Robert Tallant, a folklorist funded by the WPA to collect material in Louisiana during the Depression, preserved a verse he found in New Orleans in the 1930s that details a man's doubts and then his final decision to go for it:

> Guess what mah gal tol me de other night in bed?
> Do you know dat hoe tol me to use mah head.
> Ah tol her, baby, Ah ain't no cock sucker
> Den she whispered she knew black John Rucker.
> Den what did Ah do?
> You wouldn't want John Rucker foolin wid ya gal, would you?
> Oh, you sucked her pussy, did you?
> Man, Ah sucked dat pussy, til it was blue.

When I first came across it, I assumed the name "John Rucker" was just made up to rhyme with "sucker"—but in the recent history *Beale Street Dynasty*, Preston Lauterbach writes about a major court case in Memphis in 1868, in which a white woman was put on trial for shooting a black woman over their shared black lover, who visited when her husband was at work, and his name was Jim Rucker. It's not a long way from Jim to John, and I'm guessing there were lots of songs and rhymes about that case—none of which would have been collected or transcribed because they all would have used obvious rhymes for "Rucker." But some versions apparently survived as folklore, and seventy years later a woman could still scare a man just by mentioning that she "knew black John Rucker."

That verse is again from a male viewpoint—it suggests cunnilingus is something you might not want to do, but you have to do it to keep a woman satisfied. The verses collected from women often make that point as well, but with the notable difference that many of them add instructional tips. For example, Tallant's collection includes this verse from a female informant:

> Love is sweet as butter
> To keep a woman yo way ya got to suck her.
> When ya suck a woman an she begin to come
> Tickle her purry tongue wid ya tongue.

> An if a woman laks to fuck fast,
> Ya can git her yo way by lickin her ass.
> Dere is really an art in sucking
> De women lak it better den fuckin.

There is another good example of hidden history in that verse: there are virtually no English-language slang or colloquial terms for the clitoris—as opposed to German, or numerous African languages, which have familiar words for that organ—but three lyrics in the Tallant collection use the term "purry tongue," suggesting it was common in black New Orleans. It's a cute euphemism—a pussy has a purry tongue—but I have not found a single example of it in any other source.

That doesn't mean the term was unusual, or limited to New Orleans. Very little uncensored material survives from the early twentieth century, still less from African Americans, and less again from African American women. There is only one surviving recording of a black woman explicitly singing about oral sex in this period, Lucille Bogan's "Till the Cows Come Home"—which was recorded in 1933, but only released in 2004—and she introduces the discourse of quid pro quo, singing, "If you suck my pussy, baby, I'll suck your dick."

That kind of lyric was not intended as naughty comedy—it was the straightforward language of working people before mass media introduced new standards of middle-class propriety. However, it became increasingly submerged as the "race record" industry spread thousands of blues lyrics that cloaked their sexy themes in winking euphemisms. In 1928 a singer and guitarist named Tampa Red became one of the biggest stars on that market with a hit called "It's Tight Like That"—which carefully avoided specifying the "it" in question—and he followed up in 1929 with "What Is It That Tastes Like Gravy," a sample verse relating:

> The gal that let me taste it, they put her in jail
> She didn't need nothing to go her bail
> She had something tastes like gravy...

Ten years later, one of the biggest hits of 1939 was a song called "Hold Tight! I Want Some Seafood, Mama," first recorded by the clarinetist Sidney Bechet and quickly covered by Fats Waller and the Andrews Sisters. The lyrics referred to a yen for shrimp and oysters, and the Fishery Council of New York and the Mid-Atlantic States briefly adopted it as an advertising theme, but the real meaning was signaled by the line "when I come home late at night, I get my favorite dish: fish!" Though the Andrews Sisters professed their innocence, NBC banned the song from airplay, and when Eudora Welty wrote a short story in which a jazz musician sang it, the editors of Atlantic magazine made her substitute an alternate title.

Censorship could only reach so far, and some people undoubtedly kept trading dirty barroom rhymes, but the next wave of songs about real-life sexual practices wouldn't sweep in until the 1970s. Ike and Tina Turner provided a foretaste when they hit in 1968 with "I've Been Loving You Too Long," including a long interlude about oral sex in their live performances. This interlude is mainly remembered because Ike, in one of his most famously abusive acts, forced Tina to mime fellatio with the microphone, but what virtually no one seems to remember—perhaps because it is harder to fit into the story of their profoundly unequal relationship—is that in the middle of this sequence, Ike remarks, "Now, look-a-hear, baby, I ain't never tried anything like this here before, but I'll try anything one time," and makes his own slurping love to the mike, to which Tina responds with a moan, then a broad smile as she tells him, "Try it one more time," and begins to fake an orgasm.

The soul revolution paralleled the sexual revolution and the feminist revolution, and although those movements were not always in sync, new conversations were happening in some surprising venues. A lot of people found those conversations embarrassing, for a variety of reasons: when a singer and comedian named Blow Fly cut a dirty parody of Otis Redding's "Fa Fa Fa Fa Fa (Sad Song)" as "The Eating Song (Yum-Yum)," with lines like "She's got the only cunt that's sweet enough to eat, good tasting cunt, y'all," most people would have found it offensive for the language he was using. But he had another concern, interrupting himself to remind "the ladies" in the audience that he was just kidding: "I don't go in the bushes, speaking for myself—I don't know about the rest of the fellahs. Not yet."

That was in 1973, and the "not yet" was a nervous male response to changing mores. Four years later, Marvin Gaye testified to his recognition of those changes on "Soon I'll Be Loving You Again," singing to his young lover,

"I never did that before, but there's always a first time," while in falsetto his background vocal specified: "I never gave up no head"—and by the end of the song he was ecstatically repeating the promise: "I'm gonna give you some head."

The lushly layered disco instrumentation made it easy to miss the details of Gaye's lyric, but in 1977 Millie Jackson opened her Feelin' Bitchy album with a ten-minute track called "All the Way Lover" that made her point clear with a spoken interlude: between soaring demands for an "all the way lover," she instructed female listeners to demand that their men "get on down and partée"—a word of her own coinage, which she explained meant "no kissee on the belly button and stopping, now." She extended this commentary on a 1979 live album, adding the familiar racial dig: "It's about time you black guys caught up...it's about time y'all came on in and gave us black women what these white girls been getting!" She was working the subject for edgy comedy, but the wild applause from female listeners soon prompted her to get more serious: in 1983 she recorded a straight-up sexy soul ode to oral satisfaction called "Slow Tongue."

Like the early African American blues scene—and unlike the later, white-fan-based blues scene, which tends to consist of white guys applauding guitar virtuosos—the soul scene was aimed largely at an audience of black women. In the 1980s, as dance-oriented music took command of the national R&B market, that soul scene went south and was rebranded as "down home blues," "soul-blues," or simply blues. The stars were mostly older, second-tier soul singers, including Millie Jackson, Denise LaSalle, Clarence Carter, and Latimore (the composer of Jackson's "All the Way Lover"). At a typical southern blues show, virtually everyone in the audience is African American, and it's about 80 percent women, mostly in their forties, fifties, or sixties.

The soul-blues scene thrives on racy songs, but they are racy songs for older women—and in 1987 a forty-one-year-old ex-gospel singer named Marvin Sease took the scene by storm with a ten-minute track called "Candy Licker." Over a mellow electric guitar groove, Sease started out with a soaring confession: "I'm not ashamed no more," he sang. "I want to do the thing that your lover never did before." Over a backing track punctuated with

1. Herbenick et al., "Sexual Behavior in the United States: Results from a National Probability Sample of Men and Women ages 14–94," *Journal of Sexual Medicine* 7, 2010, p.261-3; Dodge et al., "Sexual Health among U.S. Black and Hispanic Men and Women: A Nationally Representative Study," *Journal of Sexual Medicine* 7, 2010, p.334-5.

female sighs and moans, he pled: "Let me lick you up, let me lick you down/Turn around, baby, let me lick you all around." Then, going back to his church roots, he broke from the song to deliver a spoken testimony:

> "You know what, honey? Your man ain't going down on you, girl. No— because you're man got too much pride. You know, it's funny—I used to be like that too, girl. But one day my lady told me, "Marvin, you better get your shit together, man." And girl, I started going down."

"Candy Licker" was more than just a one-off hit; it defined Sease's career. His later album titles would include *Do You Need a Licker?*, *A Woman Would Rather Be Licked*, and, most simply: *Breakfast*. I saw him perform on a multi-act blues bill at the Gibson Amphitheater in Los Angeles, and his set was almost entirely devoted to testimony about the glories of giving head, punctuated with exhortations to the overwhelmingly female audience to demand that their men do likewise. The other male singers on the bill stuck to more macho fare, but Denise LaSalle, the one female performer, made her views clear: "I don't like none of these men," she said. "Except Marvin. Marvin's OK with me."

LaSalle herself took on the subject in 2000, getting one of her biggest late-career hits with a high-powered admonishment to men that they should "treat your lady like a stamp and a letter," which set up the title line: "Lick it Before You Stick It."

A few southern blues artists bucked the trend—a singer named Roy C countered with "I'm Not Going to Eat a Thing (Unless You Put It in the Frying Pan)"—but most recognized that their audience wanted positive reinforcement and got with the program. Chuck Roberson aimed for the Sease audience with "Lollipop Man (Licking On Your Love Is My Game)," Lee Shot Williams cutting the charmingly-titled "I'm a Nibble Man," and the old-time soul man Jerry "Swamp Dogg" Williams issuing the macho threat, "If I Ever Kiss It, He Can Kiss It Goodbye." Meanwhile, on the distaff side, Big Cynthia (daughter of the Motown star Junior Walker) hit with "Eating Ain't Cheating," as well as "Don't Rock the Boat (Just the Little Man in It)," and an artist called Ms Jody came up with a variation specifically addressed to older men, "Lick If You Can't Stick," reassuring them: "Don't you feel embarrassed if you fall down on the job/ 'Cause you can still give me a thrill without that lightning rod."

Rappers, performing for an audience largely comprised of adolescent males, were more wary. In 1990, Tribe Called Quest's second single, "Bonita Applebum" had Q-Tip rapping "I'd like to kiss you where some brothers won't"—old stereotypes die hard. But when HWA (Hos with Attitude) tried to make a stronger statement the same year with the assertive "Eat It" (sample lyric: "I'm gonna take your head, lead you there/ Let your tongue part the hair"), it went nowhere.

By contrast, the female trio SWV got a Top 40 R&B in 1993 hit singing a warm retro-soul ballad about the pleasure of a man finally taking "the road to ecstasy" and going "Downtown...to taste the sweetness." The language was careful, but it proved that there was a young R&B audience ready to hear the message. In 1996 Lil Kim took an unambiguous stand on her first album with "Not Tonight." Though most of her material seemed to be aimed at an audience of sexually clueless but eager male teenagers, this song was a brief attempt to school them: As she explained, her favorite man would "Lay me on my back, bustin' nuts all in me." But after ten sessions she had only come twice and getting sick of the imbalance: "I never was pushy [but] the motherfucker never ate my pussy." Hence the straight-talking chorus: "I don't want dick tonight/ Eat my pussy right."

Some stories never seem to change: from the earliest blues to the latest rap, women keep trying to get the message across, and men keep picking up on it like it's news and acting like heroes if they pay attention. In real terms, the numbers seem to be going up—a recent survey suggests that almost 90 percent of American women in their twenties have received oral sex from a man at some point in their lives, as compared to fewer than 50 percent of women over seventy. The numbers were roughly the same for black women, and though the proportions of black men who said they'd given head to a woman were slightly lower than the average, that may be less a matter of what people do than of what they tell researchers.[1] As the New Orleans jump rapper MC E said in 1993: "They all out here frontin' like they don't do it, but we all know that they..." and then, after a dramatic tongue-slurp, the chorus line comes in: "Lick the Cat!" ✍

ELIJAH WALD *is a music historian and the author of a dozen books, most recently* Dylan Goes Electric.

Office Hours: Jeff Tweedy on the Work of Wilco

Tim Kinsella probes Jeff Tweedy on being a middle class band, creative labor and how the Monkees influenced Wilco

BY TIM KINSELLA

PHOTOGRAPHS BY DAVID C. SAMPSON

Twenty years into their run, it is not easy to contribute anything new to the conversation about what Wilco does and how it does it. This is not dissimilar to the challenges Jeff Tweedy has taken on: how to pay respect, contribute to, and expand upon his inherited traditions, while at the same time making these traditions speak for himself. It is a calling so gargantuan that only one totally at ease with himself and his place in the world could take it on gracefully. And grace is what it requires. It is a demonstration of confidence distilled of any whiff of arrogance.

His casual embodiment of multiple paradoxes situates Tweedy perfectly for this position. And it is the resolution of these many contradictions, in action, that bolsters the meaning of the ambition. If we are to take his songs as evidence, Tweedy has always been at ease with wistfulness and has kept his cool even when reeling through peaks of joy. The forms and the feels of the songs most often channel earnest Midwest sensibilities, while simultaneously dragging these traditions into The Now with contemporary flourishes.

Tweedy himself is a cultural anomaly. A down-to-earth yet daring everyman, exalted to the iconic status of the stars of classic rock, he comes across as possessing the humble work ethic of a John Cougar Mellencamp or Neil Young while also having the big-eared avant-savvy to enlist collaborators like Jim O'Rourke, Nels Cline, and Darin Gray. His songs dignify universal themes: love, love lost, frustration, the struggles of growth. Taken together, they breezily proclaim a faith that personal hardship can be overcome with hard work. Delivered with the perfect degree of twang and strain, the words consistently hold just enough wisdom to fill each song to capacity without ever overbearing it.

The simple strum and boogie that unifies a great amount of Wilco's songs can almost appear as a series of variations to stake a claim as heir to the shuffling mournful swagger of "Tom Thumb's Blues." No one since Big Star has made such expansive diversity within traditional forms appear so effortless. This eclecticism is always about resolution instead of juxtaposition, and this is what makes their wide vocabulary come across as so perfectly American.

Tweedy's work ethic as a craftsman is consistent with this feel of the songs. They appear as evidence of his noble ambition, perfecting the inherited form. And we trust him. When he struggles to express himself, we trust the struggle is real because we understand there are no fronts. Part of what makes him so believable is the sense that none of what he does is impossible. It comes across as a hard-won talent rather than some rare God-given gift. We trust new songs will already be familiar even while they challenge or stun us with their attention to ornamentation. People criticize Wilco for being safe, but what they actually are is dependable, a virtue.

But however at ease he may come across as a man, as a performer, and as the narrators in his songs, Tweedy is a craftsman constantly challenging himself to sharpen and clarify the expanding outer ends of the spectrum of his sound. The challenge of being Jeff Tweedy these days might be how to keep a good thing going. How to keep his Big Star expanding while its center maintains its integrity?

In person, in conversation, his easy-going forthrightness is disarming, personifying both clear-headedness and youthful excitement.

—TIM KINSELLA

Do you keep office hours here at the loft?

I don't know if I would call them office hours, but I do feel like coming into this amazing environment that I've managed to be able to put together in my life, to come be in it even when I don't have something I need to do, is more likely to result in something I'm excited about than if I was just sitting on my ass. I like to go to work. I might just come up and write.

Are you always writing?

I really believe at this point in my life that I am always writing, that people who write are always writing no matter what they're doing. Some part of my brain is always writing, and it can be a little distracting.

Distracting to real life?

Just to living.

Do you put in a forty-hour work week?

Most weeks would be more than that, I think. It's been a long time since I haven't been working on something when I'm not on the road, either someone else's record or demos for Wilco or putting together the Tweedy record with Spencer. Those days can be anywhere from 12 to 3, when there's something like real life I have to do, or they can end up being 12 to 12, just a whole day.

Are you aware consciously of discipline versus inspiration, then? Maybe it doesn't feel like discipline if you're excited to wake up and come here to the loft, anyway.

I've always been a pretty firm believer in the notion that younger artists wait around for inspiration and, at some point, artists just decide to go to work. That's where I'm at. Fortunately, at this point in my life after doing this for a long time, I feel more excited about it, more energized to do it, and more appreciative that I get to do it than I did when I was younger and didn't understand just how exalted you are in your life to actually even find something you love to do.

What role does playfulness have in all of this?

It's all playfulness. I think it's very little execution. I was making the analogy the other day that a lot of my process is like making a paper snowflake. You just keep cutting at it and you don't know what it's gonna look like exactly. You just blindly kind of do, and know that the reveal is going to happen at some point and it's not gonna hurt anybody if it's terrible or embarrassing. But more often than not, it's just like, "Wow! How did *that* happen?" I'm the happiest with the end result the more time I can spend without my ego being involved.

If you're always recording, always writing, at what point are you aware of the overall form of a record, of the thing that binds the songs?

One of the advantages of having this place is that I can work on something and put it away for two months and then get to hear it again with fresh ears and go, "Woah, I like that," or "I didn't realize that was as bad as that is." That's the whole point of writing everyday and not reading it. It's basically an exercise that I think every good writer learns how to do. You turn it off and then on again and then you can kind of read it like you're the audience. But a lot of times I'll be surprised by a batch of songs that I had forgotten about. Wilco's worked a lot of different ways together, all sitting in a circle and hammering out twelve songs and all the arrangements. I'll bring a song in, but nothing beyond a chord structure and some lyrics. Most recently, I've taken just really, really raw snippets of songs and then put them in a sequence or a shape that I think would make an interesting record.

Let's say it's ten songs. How many full ten-song records?

There are three that I've been playing around with. One is mostly a catchall. I've just started doing this with stuff that's a little bit more...things that have been approached at least once.

By the rest of the band?

Or myself with Spencer. Stuff we've tried to refine at least one time, like, *Let's see if these songs fit together.* I've been doing that for a long time. I'm glad you asked me that. I used to have a dictaphone cassette recorder and it just lived on the coffee table in Sue and my apartment. I would do an acoustic guitar song and then I would put it away, come back a day or two later, listen to what I'd done and think, "What comes next on the record?" I wrote all of *Being There* like that. But every time, I would start by listening to the whole thing up until the point of the next song.

How does collaboration work with Wilco?

It's worked in different ways at different times. Everybody is really busy outside of the band, which I think is always kind of a hidden secret, having longevity and having a fairly gratified and appreciative environment to work in. Everybody's out doing something smaller in a van and then, like, "I can't believe we still get to get on a bus and do this."

Why do you think that benefits you all?

I think everybody benefits musically from being a musician [*laughs*], and not just feeling like they have to express themselves through Wilco or bringing things back to Wilco that they've learned to do in other environments. But, because of that, it's been a little bit more me working alone in the last couple of years. No two records have had exactly the same process, and I think that makes it more exciting.

The other members don't have office hours in the same kind of way. Do you call them in at a certain point?

We schedule time when we're all gonna be here, and that's harder and harder to do with the amount of outside activity in the band, myself included. Spencer and I spent the last year or so touring around doing the Tweedy record stuff, but yeah, it's a relatively new thing. The last record, *The Whole Love*, we got together in a couple of big chunks of time, maybe a total of a month of everybody being in one place, but then I'm left to my own devices to edit it and finish it. The one I'm finishing I think would benefit a lot from sounding like there had been no consideration.

How do you mean that?

It was just a record that was made in two days and nobody had time to decide whether the guitar solo was good or not, or whether those lyrics were worth singing. I think the last couple of Wilco records have been *really* manicured and really "OK, this is what we do and we are really good at doing this thing and let's do that because it's still

fun to do." I think over time, a band that has been around a long time... I don't know, I just get bummed out when I see a band that's been around a long time making records that feel like they're still thinking, *This is the big one*.

Did you ever see that Ramones documentary? There's this moment, they're being interviewed on Mexican television in 1993 and they're saying, "Now that alternative music has hit, this is our big break!" It's such a bummer. It's like, "Oh, man, you're the Ramones!"

I mean, I want every record to do as well as it can do. By the end of a record, though, I don't think I've ever put out a record I didn't feel like, *That's something I couldn't have made five years ago*.

What's the standard by which you want each one to do as well as it can do? You mean in terms of sales and the scale of its reach, or just all of it?

I've always wanted every record to have a chance to reach people that I wouldn't necessarily like. Do you know what I mean? I think that's a good cause!

I think that's an amazing ambition.

Not that I have this gospel to spread or something.

I mean, it's an incredibly generous way of thinking about it, but I'm curious.

Well, I don't know. Who am I to judge? Just because I don't like 'em doesn't mean that I'm in a position that I should be able to judge them for their musical taste. I always look at a lot of bands, and all these indie bands in Chicago—bands I've known over the years that I have a lot of respect for and care about—I've always felt they're trying to pick their audience, trying to make their audience be as cool as they are. I've always thought that was bullshit in a way. I don't really care. I've never been cool.

I have these old friends who I toured with a lot, playing similar-sized shows. One year to the next, they're playing to much bigger audiences, and I asked my friend how he felt about it. He was like, "It's pretty strange. Suddenly, there's all kinds of people I wouldn't be friends with seeing us."

There was always the debate about being on a major label or not being on a major label in the '90s. My argument was that I wouldn't be interested in music if it wasn't for major labels. All my favorite bands when I was a little kid came to me because this apparatus was built by a bunch of horrible people, granted, but that's how I was saved from a lot of misery. And I certainly was, at the very least, consoled, so that argument's a fucking flatout no way for me, right off the bat. Like, *Does that mean I have to go and crawl across cut glass when they appeal to my ambition?*

What do you mean?

When they're like, "Just do this and you guys are gonna be big stars." No, but I wanna use your distribution.

How aware are you, then, during the writing process, of the audience?

Completely unaware. That's the other side of it, too. I can say that I don't wanna make any decisions about who's gonna listen to it, but that's because I don't feel confident enough that I know who's gonna like it.

Do you ever make a choice where you're like, "Ah, this is getting too weird"?

No, I wanna make myself happy. I just want it to be almost as cool as my favorite stuff.

That's the standard? *Almost* as cool?

[*laughs*] Well, it's always gonna be, it'll never be as cool.

How's it sound when you hear yourself, when you hear an old record? Not when you're re-learning an old song to play, but, like, when you walk into a café.

It's generally uncomfortable, like if I'm listening through stuff with my kids or something. If they're like, "I've never heard Uncle Tupelo. Let's listen to it," I'm generally kind of wistful about it. I'm like, *Wow, that's not so bad*. But it's always kind of obsolete to me once the record comes out and the world has a chance to ruin it. Once I'm done with it I don't have any control over that, and that's kind of what we're talking about. I think a lot of people I've seen over the years, to varying degrees of pathology, are so dis-

tracted by this idea that they can control what happens to their music once it's out into the world. I feel sorry for them because they have *no* control over it, so they're always gonna be disappointed.

Saying that all the records that saved you, or at least consoled you and brought you to music, and then you do have access to the same infrastructure and distribution networks—

I did. I guess I still do, but I'm a little bit more autonomous.

Either way, has that affected the process at all, that shift in business?

I don't think so. I think that early on, before we were off of a major label, we had already started affording ourselves freedoms that we probably hadn't earned. To be perfectly frank, nobody was really paying attention to us anyway. Nobody was micromanaging, or even managing, what we were doing. Up to the time we made *Yankee Hotel Foxtrot*, nobody ever looked at me and thought, "That dude's gonna be a sensation." [The record label] thought they didn't have to do anything. A lot of bands would've told you at that time to take the most money you can take because then they'll care about you, they'll wanna follow up on their investment, but that was never comfortable to me, and we were never really offered huge chunks of money anyway.

This is kind of an impossible question, but Wilco as it exists now—could it have ever been this, in your mind, fifteen years ago?

I think it's actually really close to what I had in my mind all the way back to Uncle Tupelo. I always wanted a collective of friends who I could play music with. I've always romanticized it in a sincere and naïve way that that was just an awesome thing to get to do with men in your life! You have your girlfriend or you have your wife, and over time, you have these intimate things with women and you get to have that in your life, but men are a lot more shy about having an intimate environment to be together in. And to work together in music, I think, is a really beautiful, intimate environment. Not that if a woman was in the group I would feel any different.

This is a really interesting twist on the normalized

TIM KINSELLA

"Contrary to the critical shorthand for my career, that I like firing people, I think I've actually let things go longer than they should've just because I was really committed to the idea of a band."

—Jeff Tweedy

version of a band being a group of men. Is it that being in a band creates a way for there to be an intimate space between men that they're comfortable with?

That's kind of what I'm getting at. I always spent a lot more time with my mom when I was younger, so I've always been inherently a lot more comfortable around women, a lot more confident, at least. I had two brothers that were much older than I am, so I think there was a lot that was un-understood—just no way to comprehend, at that age, resentment or jealousy, being the baby, the exalted little kid that just came along ten years after. That's the environment I feel like I grew up in. I looked at the Monkees and *A Hard Day's Night* and *Help!* and thought, "Oh, man, that's how guys are supposed to be together. They're all in it *together*. That's awesome!"

So what sort of lineage, then, are you aware of? Are there multiple lineages in your head, one that you feel Wilco and you are carrying on a tradition of?

Do you mean do we think we're carrying on the Monkees' aesthetic? The Monkees' interpersonal dynamic? That actually *is* closer to what I would've pictured it at a very young age. [When Uncle Tupelo broke up], I was really blindsided. *Why would you wanna quit? This is amazing! It's just getting good.* And then, over time, I think I've allowed less functional dynamics to exist longer than they needed to. Contrary to the critical shorthand for my career, that I like firing people, I think I've actually let things go longer than they should've just because I was really committed to the *idea* of a band.

It's different than just a band-as-clubhouse, because the very simple fact is that you are here working every day and you are making these choices.

Well, it's always been my band. When Uncle Tupelo broke up, *I* was given a record contract with my name on it to sign. The label wasn't as interested in having a band sign a contract, and Jay [Farrar] got a contract, too. I think they just hung on to me 'cause they could, 'cause I was already under contract: *Let's just see what happens.* From that point on, it's been my responsibility and in everyone's best interest for me to hopefully not steer the ship into

the ground. I've gotten more and more comfortable with that over the years. I feel more confident than I did fifteen years ago that that's OK.

With that confidence in how you steer the ship, is there also a greater confidence in how much of yourself is in the songs?

I think that my goal is to not to fuck up whatever spell is being cast by the music. In some song structures, some music environments lead to more direct expression, and some lead to more hiding, just letting the sounds be more of a part of it.

And you're equally comfortable with either of those, depending on the song?

I am. I'm excited when a really crystallized idea comes through really clearly in a song, but I won't let it stop me from finishing it [if that doesn't happen]. I'm not gonna wait around for it. Sometimes something'll just come out really clear. Sometimes it'll make me cry: *Oh, wow, I didn't have any idea that that was going to be so blunt.* Then there are other times where I'm like, *I still don't know why I'm singing these words, but they sure feel good to sing.* Like they sure feel like what belongs there, but I haven't quite unlocked why that is. And they're equally satisfying, I think. If i had my choice, I would probably want everything to land as strongly as something super clear, but I also realize that there are tons of songs I love that I don't have any clue what the lyrics are, despite listening to them a thousand times.

It seems like those two ways of approaching the lyrics are actually two different ways of approaching the songs. The clear ones being, "I am expressing something to the world," but with the others are you learning about yourself, surprising yourself. Do you learn about yourself through songs?

[*Laughs.*] No. No, I think that's the beauty of it. I think I know myself very well. I think I've had to get to know myself very well to be healthier in my life. And I think that it really all ends up being acceptance of the parts of me that just come out. And because I'm not hiding them or I'm not making myself... I don't know, sing macho lyrics. I'm not making myself sing... I don't know. [*pause*] I look at a lot of bands and I wonder why they're yelling. Like, *Why are you angry, man?* [*laughs.*] I know they're, like, not even angry, they're singing love songs, but they're belting. I don't know. Anyway, I digress. Mumford and Sons on *SNL* the other night, did you see that?

I didn't see it.

They're like, screaming. I don't know why... Why was I talking about that?

We were talking about whether you surprise yourself. I mean, you said it's about filters. And you're talking about things seeming true because you're not putting any kind of false filter on them.

I don't wanna make it sound like I bravely go deep into my subconscious and I come back with this stuff. No. I think it's just really simply a gratifying and pleasing thing to me to make something that wasn't there. And by the time that happens, that's served its purpose for me. I can take a little bit of pride over the years at getting better at sharing that, putting that into a context, like we've been talking about a lot, that's more audible or visible or evident, that this person knows how to put a song together. But the process is really what has sustained me, what has made me happy.

All right, so here's the big question about dealing with [your son] Spencer. As a father, there's various roles. As we've been talking about, there's all sorts of tricks for bouncing your own sense of intuition and craftsmanship, but the simple fact is that you've been doing this a lot longer than he has. So there must be a lot of shortcuts. Right? I mean in terms of craftsmanship.

No. He's better than I am. [*laughs*] He's a much better musician than I am. He is! He's a much more naturally confident and gifted musician. He's a kid, but he's very smart and very astute, and a lot of what I would be able to teach him is just going to come through from proximity.

Like he's absorbed it over the years?

Well, yeah, and also just from experience. The biggest thing I could give him is an opportunity to play with other people, to play with Darin Gray, somebody who's just gonna kick his ass. And he kind of kicked all of our asses.

Darin Gray?

No, Spencer. He's by far and away the most consistently spot-on musician on stage every night.

What about In terms of putting songs together? Maybe i'm revealing something about my own relationship with my dad...

Inevitably you are. But, well. I'm going to interview you the rest of the way.

[laughs] But, there's a sort of asymmetry.

The only thing that I may have provided a shortcut to is when he starts to overthink or get neurotic. We're all sensitive beings. People who gravitate toward this type of expression or this type of life or who have immersed themselves in creating and in art—we're very sensitive people. And just reassuring him that it's okay. There's way worse things in life than not feeling good.

What about your own dad, did you have some shared activity with him?

Nah. I wasn't allowed to touch his tools.

So it wasn't normalized in any way.

My dad is still alive. When he worked, he worked on the railroad, and like a lot of railroad people, he was very much married to the railroad—on call twenty-four hours a day. We maybe took one family vacation my entire childhood. He worked all the time, woke up at three in the morning. The thing I wanted to do—I joked with my dad that he gave me a lot of great parental advice because whenever I think, *What would my dad do?* it is invariably the right thing to do the opposite. Like, would my dad go to this school play? *No.* So I should go. But in all seriousness, later in life I thought it was weird that I couldn't picture my dad at work. What was he doing? I went to the railroad once with him, but I couldn't put together in my mind what his day was like. And I think early on, it was important to Susie and I that when I call from the road and say, "I'm at soundcheck," they can picture soundcheck.

And you were aware of that.

TIM KINSELLA

Yeah. I wanted them to be able to picture me, and where I was. When I say, "Oh, I'm in the dressing room, we're playing a big theatre tonight," they know, "Oh, big theatre, I've been to the Vic" or whatever. I think that's helped a lot, with traveling and the amount of time I've spent gone, and making them feel, over the years, that I haven't been gone as much. Throughout their lives I've probably been gone a third of every year. We averaged over a hundred shows a year for twenty years. 180 shows a year, some years. Always kind of on tour.

Susie's an incredible mom, and has done an amazing job keeping our kids alive. If I could say anything for myself, it is that I'm still so connected to a childlike kind of existence. I've been doing this for almost thirty years. I've been allowed to *play* for a long time. What do I do? I come here and play. I'm still playing. I think that has allowed me to be on their level a lot. And empathetic.

Are there lessons that you're returning to over and over? For example, Bad Brains and Bauhaus are two bands I've spent almost thirty years listening to now—yet they are always different, my hearing of them changes.

My listening habits are really much more fluid than that. I'll listen to a song again and again after that initial listening, and often I'm like, "What the fuck is going on? How is this happening?" A lot of records don't hold up over time, either because I've gotten better as a musician to the point where I can hear...

You're no longer impressed.

I think so. Yeah. Like, *They just kinda shat that out.* Mark and I were talking about this the other day. A lot of bands, in the '80s and '90s, their records were terrible, but the experience of seeing them was so great. What the world has made has ruined it... The mystery is gone of what they were. You thought they were real vampires or some other type of being that could make this music. But really they were just some guys who could barely play the bass and had a chorus pedal.

With your own records, do you want people to hear the labor?

"Labor" implies that it was not fun. The last few records were really fun to make, but highly considered. The consideration that was happening was very detail oriented but ultimately satisfying in its own way. Something has shifted in the last couple of years when it's been like, I can't imagine enjoying that as much.

Are old records not holding up because you're listening for those details? I'm not trying to...contradiction is the test of realism.

Well, an artist is someone who can hold two opposing viewpoints with equal conviction.

Yes. So my question is whether there's a difference between playing at the limits. The tension when you can tell that someone is playing at the absolute limits of their ability, and it's not very good in a technical sense, can be powerful. But when someone's faking that, it comes across.

It eventually shines through, yeah. Inspired amateurism, to me, is the ideal state of rock n' roll.

We can't all be the Shaggs. The worst thing, I feel like, that one can say of a band, is that it's less than the sum of its parts. The best thing is that mysterious aura, like, I know exactly how they're doing this, but how are they doing this?

That's the trick a lot of people can't get to, in the studio. Allowing a mistake. Everybody talks about it, "Oh, it's a happy accident!" No. There's a difference between Led Zeppelin turning the beat around and having it sound intentional, versus you accidentally hitting the wrong chord and it somehow working. I don't know what it is exactly, but it's liberation.

Is it the confidence of knowing that the thing itself is strong enough to hold? Like, think Astral Weeks. Those people obviously don't know how to play the songs.

They've never been allowed to know how to play the songs.

Right. I remember the Mojo article coming out about the making of it on the anniversary, and everyone they interviewed who played on it said

"I think that my goal is to not to fuck up whatever spell is being cast by the music."

—Jeff Tweedy

they'd never met Van Morrison. He was just, like, in another room.

He was such a horrible person to be around that they weren't letting the other musicians in... You know my wife, right?

Yeah, yeah, a little bit. I was really young when I was at Lounge Ax all the time. Like, nineteen, twenty?

Oh. [*laughs*.] She let you in?

There was a good amount of people there that I still know and see around. I was a really shy little guy. It was just intense. I had a fake ID.

We were going to St. Louis when we were kids, to see punk rock shows, and we'd be doing our best to look like we belonged, with very limited information about what that entailed. I remember wearing a bandana around my waist one time. Like, *Is this punk?* And then getting there and, you know, pulling the bandana out. The real punks all had it down and they knew where to get Doc Martens. There weren't any Doc Martens in Belleville.

How far is Belleville from St. Louis?

It's not that far, but it might as well be on the other side of the moon.

Pre-internet. It feels like a different world to me. When the phones all stayed in one place. And you had to have the skills to say something like, "Hi, this is Tim, is Jeff there?" The cycles were very clear: We're writing now, we're doing promo now, we're touring now. That's a technological shift that creates a cultural shift.

I talk about this all the time. Whenever you get together with old-timers, inevitably, it's like, "How did we survive? How did we actually get to the gig?" You had a map, you had to find a payphone, you had to call the asshole who ran the bar, and they wouldn't be very helpful. I was telling Steve Albini the other day, I wanna start a band with him where we only use '80s technology for touring.

I just think that for everybody, for all of the hand-wring-

ing over the music business, I just think it's fucking better now. Everything about it is better, from my perspective. And it's not because we've had success. [Artists] have access to recording equipment, they have access to an audience, you know? There's a lot to compete with, but they have access. That's why it's democratized in a lot of ways. There's a tribe for everybody, pretty much. If you become interested in a type of music, it's all at your fingertips. That can be good or bad. Maybe some people appreciated it more when they had to go digging through record crates for it, but in general, there are a lot of things that are so much more realistic. It would have been awesome to have Bandcamp when I started. You know? It would have been really fun.

It would've been a totally different thing though. Because removing finding the secret...the way things were treasured...

I think there were a lot of bands then that just disappeared because they never had anybody with any wherewithal to get to the first step of making a cassette and sending it to somebody.

Were there ambitions or ideas you had at the beginning that you're still aware of, that you kind of hold close and aspire to?

By the time Uncle Tupelo got a van and drove to Columbia, Missouri, and played a gig at the Blue Note, we'd achieved almost all the things we'd had ambition to do. Everything else since then has been like, *OK, now this is happening.* Like, *We never saw any shows in a place like this. So...how do you play in a place like this? I guess we have to get better at it, because people are coming to see us in a place like this.* Same with festivals. I never went to see festivals or arena shows. But we've played arenas and stuff. So I was like, "Oh, what do you do? How do I make this feel right for us to do?" Is it my ideal situation to play music in? No. But I look at it as a kind of challenge. Like, *Can we reach the back row?*

Are you this optimistic with everything?

[*laughs.*]

I get picked on a lot for my unrelenting optimism... People will be like, "Dude, that's not what's happening." I'm like, "This seems pretty good!"

Susie laughs at me when I say I'm an optimist. I think I'm really pessimistic about people. I really hate people.

I'm pretty sure you don't. The little bits you've revealed about your attitude toward the common man...

I think the difference is that I hate myself more for hating them. I don't want to hate people. My inclination is definitely optimistic. I don't wanna feel like I'm smarter than anybody or, I don't know, that people are bad or they have bad intentions. I really don't. We were just on vacation in Mexico, and the pool was full of spring-breakers, and it was like *American Splendor*—I wanted to kill everybody. I couldn't stand how awful everyone was.

Are they all like, "I'm pretty sure that's Jeff Tweedy shaking his fist at us."

Oh, no. Complete anonymity. For sure.

That must not happen often.

It happens all the time. I don't think...

You feel free to walk into a coffee shop?

Absolutely. Maybe it's just a general indication of the goodwill people seem to feel toward me or vice versa—people don't bother me. You're worse off when you have a fucking security guard, or an entourage, and you make a big show of wherever you go. I'm not at that level of fame, but I wonder if people at that level would have a more comfortable existence if they just didn't participate in it. I have some friends who are fairly famous, and the ones who are happiest are the ones who aren't caught up in it.

I remember watching a Barry White Behind the Music a few years ago, and it turns out Barry White and Wink Martindale were BFFs. I couldn't figure it out. I thought, It's weird that famous people become friends with each other. But then it's not weird, because they don't intimidate each other. Everyone else feels weird around them.

There's a certain, I think, comfort with other people who

have that in their lives, as something to contend with that's good and bad. Another person who has some modicum of success in those terms. I feel like, for myself, I like being around somebody where I don't get any inclination at all that they want what I have, or that I shouldn't have what I have, or that they should have what I have.

Are you serious? I'm like, I wish more people liked my ideas!

Or my neighbor walking up and going, "Hey, you know what? I noticed you coming out at eight o'clock every morning, taking your kids to school. It's almost like you're a normal guy!" Like, *Yeah, I'm a normal guy*. People don't have any comprehension of it.

Right. But it must be a thing you have to take into account, moving through the world.

I'm actually fairly startled when it happens. My kids are usually more aware of it than I am when it happens. Like, "Dad, that guy is gonna come up to you." And I'm like, "Who? Where? What?" The weirdest thing was when people used to come up and talk to the kids before they'd talk to me. 'Cause they knew enough about me to know the kids' names.

Ugh.

That's the only few times I've really kinda upset my kids, 'cause I'm like, "You should just go the fuck away."

Is that the worst example of something with your unique status?

[*laughs.*] No, I can't say that's the worst. I think the worst is people who are maybe not stable, who become infatuated with you and hang out outside the club and throw rocks at the dressing room window. You just become a *thing* to people. Even really smart people, really well-adjusted people, something about fame and celebrity does crazy thing to some people, and you can't ever be this thing they've projected onto you. You just can't give it to them.

I felt much more comfortable in my life when I got to the point where I feel the same onstage as offstage. I feel like the same guy when I'm playing with Spencer as I do when I'm playing with Wilco. That's been good for me. Because

TIM KINSELLA

I've gone away and come home to my family—making that transition has always felt much better to me, feeling rooted in that and comfortable with that. I watch people who have these personas and myths that they spend a lot of time manicuring, and I just have never had the energy for that. At the same time, I do have that because, no matter how normal you feel on and off the stage, there's a certain amount of persona projected onto you just by getting up there.

There's this amazing moment in *Don't Look Back*, that scene where they're all hanging out in the hotel room, Bob Dylan's kinda holding court, and someone knocks on the door and is like, "It's time." He's just been having conversations with people. And he goes, "Oh, OK." And he opens the door and there's 10,000 people waiting there. There's no transition, but it's still all persona. It's really intense.

Because he's always on, onstage and offstage, especially at that point in his life.

You seem so excited with where you're at with everything right now. Is there a sense that this needs to end somehow, or that you'll know when you'll need to wind down?

No... I look at myself, at this point... I've spent a lot of time with Mavis [Staples], I just made a record with Richard Thompson—people who have been around a long time—and I identify with them. I identify with Mavis and people from other generations, they just wanna *do it*. I don't see any reason why I'd wanna stop doing it. Although there may be times when I feel like being home more. We've had a really intense year. Susie had a cancer diagnosis, and we've gone through treatments; I was going on tour with Tweedy and coming home for treatments. Some of the optimism and appearing to be very content and happy with where I am is probably a reflection of *Wow, that was close*. You know? We've gotten through it and the prognosis is good, so in general not too much is depressing to me about music.

You're not saying it's the conscious judo of It's been a rough year, I'd better look at the positive. You're just saying there's a great enough sense of relief?

I just think that the more real life I've had to contend with,

the more this side of things has been mostly positive. Because it becomes so petty to dwell upon, there not being a can of peanuts instead of mixed nuts in the dressing room. Whatever bullshit. It's mostly bullshit. It's the greatest thing in the world to get to do, surrounded by tons of bullshit. And it's always been that way. It always will be that way. I've managed to carve out this little thing that allows me to do it in a fairly comfortable, autonomous way. I don't look around and see a lot of middle-aged, middle-class bands. Wilco is a middle-class band. How many other middle-class bands are there? There really aren't many. There are a lot of young bands, a lot of little bands, and a lot of superstars. But there's still some of us out there, like Yo La Tengo, and Flaming Lips—it's a hard thing to do.

It's a very American thing, though. Everyone sort of feels like they're middle class. My band can tour and play to one hundred people every night and be like, "We're middle class here." But it's like, middle class is everyone making $12,000 to $70,000 a year or something.

I hope that doesn't make me sound like I'm not self-aware.

No, you sound very appreciative.

On a sliding scale, I'm probably upper middle class. But it's actually the fact of being around for twenty years that is more rare. The only real drag to me, at all, is feeling like you're getting better at something and at the same time being forced by the world to compete with yourself. Dragging this trail of records behind you, that just is always gonna be something that has spent more time in somebody's life... You can't compete with that. You can't compete with all the moments they've spent with your records. You just have to stop. ✍

TIM KINSELLA *is an author and bandleader of Joan of Arc. He lives in Chicago.*

Ice Cube and his mom in Inglewood, California, in 1990.
PHOTO BY JANETTE BECKMAN

ART BY BETH HOECKEL